Concord in the Days of
Strawberries and Streetcars

We express gratitude for the interest
shown and financial support given by
the following corporations:

Digital Equipment
Nuclear Metals
Spaulding and Company
GenRad Foundation
Welch Foods
Environmental Research and Technology
Concord Lumber
Winstanley Associates
Concord Oil
Sentry Insurance

Concord in the Days of Strawberries and Streetcars

Renee Garrelick

With a Contributing Chapter
on the Immigrant Experience by
William M. Bailey

The Town of Concord
Concord Historical Commission

Concord, Massachusetts   1985

© copyright 1985 by the Town of Concord

ISBN 0-9614575-0-3

Library of Congress Catalog Card Number 85-050267

Book Design by David Ford

Cover Illustration. The Concord, Maynard, and Hudson streetcar waits in the early morning hours on the Milldam, 1918. (Collection of the Concord Historical Commission)

This book is dedicated with affection
to those Concordians
who have lived through these years
and to those who follow.

Contents

Preface

The occasion of Concord's 350th birthday comes as the twentieth century approaches its close. Both events sparked the publication of *Concord in the Days of Strawberries and Streetcars,* a topical portrayal of community life during the earlier days of this century as told through the memories of the town's long-time residents. The book is the Concord Historical Commission's contribution to the 350th celebration.

This project has been urged ever since the oral history program began under the auspices of the Concord Historical Commission eight years ago, but the task always seemed an insurmountable one and the preferred route was to continue interviewing. Now over eighty interviews later, and with the awareness that so much material would have to be left out to fit the confines of space, time, and printing costs, the project has become a reality. We hope this book will be regarded as a testament to a town and to an era.

As the twentieth century entered its final quarter, the Concord Historical Commission recognized the need to let those people who have lived through the earlier years tell the story of their town. With the passing of time and people, many worthwhile memories had already been lost.

Through the different topic areas of recollection, the fabric of earlier twentieth-century life begins to be woven. Individuals speak of major events and of the "little things" that formed the day-to-day life style of an era. I have never left an interview without being moved and caring for the person. Ordinary people have a way of becoming very special and the human impact of such living history remains strong.

I have served as an interested listener and student of history, all the time learning from the rich diversity of Concord's population. How very precious the sound of their voices will be years from now. To all those who contributed in some way to the oral history program, whether or not their thoughts have been included for formal attribution within this publication, we express our gratitude. It is pleasing compensation that no recollections taken will be lost, as the recorded memories of the participants and the transcripts are available for public use at the Concord Free Public Library.

Oral history as a valuable primary or firsthand source of information takes on greater meaning when the principles of the historical method are applied. Information obtained from a single primary source is regarded to have possible accuracy; when obtained from two independent primary sources, a probable degree of truth; and as the number of such independent primary sources increase in confirmation, then the information obtained has greater certainty of approaching fact. When further corroborated by supplemental town records and period photos, the information offered becomes an even stronger part of the historical record.

Local residents have become acquainted with the oral history program through photo exhibits at the Concord Free Public Library; a group memory swap series; newspaper articles that I have written for the *Concord Journal;* and the programs and talks that I have had the opportunity, as the invited guest of local community groups and the schools, to present over the years.

From the inception of the oral history program, the Concord Free Public Library has housed the growing number of tapes and photographs. We are thankful to Director of the Concord Free Public Library, Rosemary Mitten, Curator Marcia Moss, and Special Collections Librarian Joyce Woodman for the attention they have shown to the needs of the program as they have watched it grow over the years.

This publication, as the oral history program itself, belongs to the Town of Concord, and we have worked closely with Town Manager Steven Sheiffer and Assistant Town Manager Anita Tekle. The special interest they have shown in this project emanates from their recognition of the importance of the human dimension to town government and their understanding of the ongoing personal outreach that the oral history program has with residents of the community.

As former chairmen of the Concord Historical Commission, Louisa McKown and Mary Wilinsky did much to nurture and encourage the oral history program in its formative years. And William Sullivan as chairman of the Historical Commission during the preparation of this book has continued this advocacy and support.

It was Eleanor Fenn, one of the first members of the Historical Commission, who pushed strongly for the formation of an oral history program for Concord. I am pleased that by the time of her death in August 1978, she was able to see the program well underway. The Historical Commission began a private fund in her memory to support the cost of conducting an oral history program beyond the amount that the town could allocate.

As an advisor to this book and a former member of the Commission, David Little has known the oral history program from its beginning. He has been a steadfast friend ever since, the one we have depended on to hang our exhibits, moderate our memory swap series, and regale audiences with his witty and moving stories about the town he knows and loves so well. We are pleased to include a number of these remembrances along with his own writing about the rivers of Concord. It has been David's sound advice that the book seek to portray a flavor of earlier twentieth-century town life, but not be encyclopedic in trying to tell it all and include everyone interviewed, that has pushed me forward with this project.

Bill Bailey will be able to chalk up to experience the major effort involved in chairing the book committee, which included raising funds for publication. He has written as well the chapter on Concord's ethnic experience. His special interest as a member of the Historical Commission in conducting oral histories of the local immigrant experience has contributed immeasurably to the program. The photo portraits taken by Alice Moulton show us the faces of many of our oral history participants, providing a lasting visual component to the program. Alice has generously donated her professional time and materials. In recognition of her contribution, the Historical Commission presented an exhibition of her photographs during its tenth anniversary commemoration at the Concord Free Public Library in April 1983.

Earlier photos of town life have become not only an indispensable part of the historical record, but also arouse strong interest and feeling when shown. We have drawn upon period photos from the collections of the Concord Free Public Library, the Department of Public Works, and the many residents who have done so much to expand our town's "family album." Peter Orlando has worked with care in reproducing these photographs, and I have valued his assistance with their selection for this book.

Whether transcribing tapes or typing manuscript, the dependable work of Nancy McKinney has given us a fighting chance to meet deadlines. We are thankful as well for the efforts of Jane Benes in preparing the index and for the interest she has shown in the development of this publication.

In such an all-consuming project as this, the families of those involved deserve a line of appreciation for their fortitude. This line, then, belongs to my family for their endurance, understanding, and above all for their love.

Renee Garrelick, Coordinator
Concord Oral History Program
Concord, Massachusetts 1984

My appreciation of those Concordians who agreed to be interviewed for the chapter "The Immigrant Experience" is boundless. Their sensitivity to my research created a strong bond of friendship. A number of people were especially helpful in contacting many Concord residents I interviewed. I am grateful in this regard to William and Mary Anderson, Charles Comeau, Mary Sheehan Dalton, Michele Lombardo, Anna Goulding Manion, and Domenica Scimone. I thank Renee Garrelick for her inspiration and support; Marcia Moss and Joyce Woodman for their assistance at the Concord Free Public Library; David Little and Clare Nunes for their editorial assistance; and Dann Chamberlin, Social Studies teacher in the Concord Middle School, who shared his extensive Concord census research with me. I regret that I was not able to reach many Concordians who undoubtedly could have added new dimensions to the story of immigration and apologize for any errors of fact or misunderstandings.

William M. Bailey
Chairman, History Department
Concord Academy
Concord, Massachusetts 1984

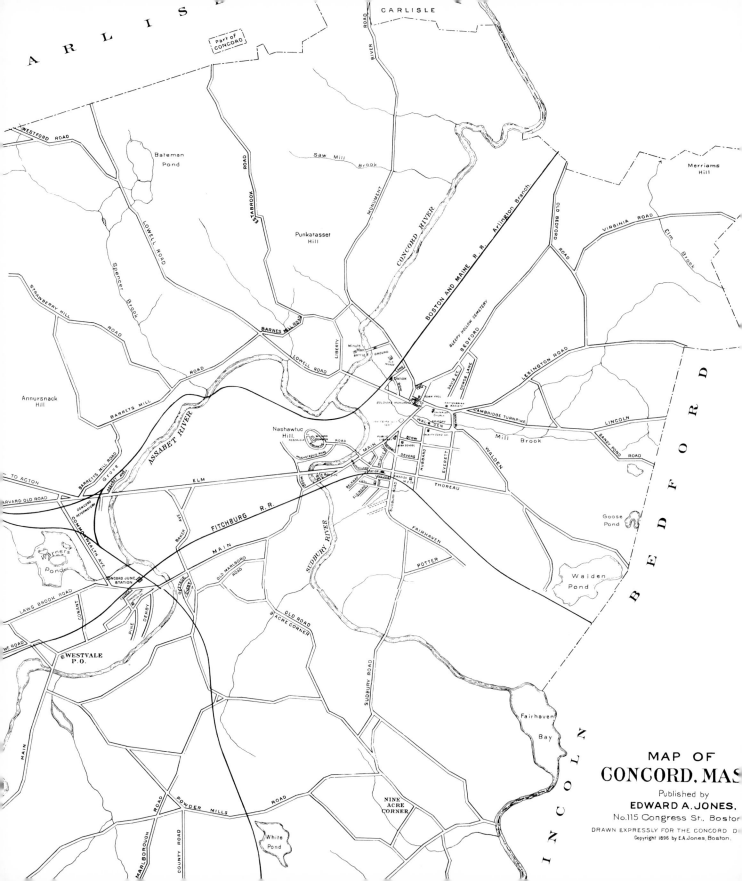

MAP OF
CONCORD, MAS
Published by
EDWARD A. JONES,
No.115 Congress St., Boston
DRAWN EXPRESSLY FOR THE CONCORD D
Copyright 1896 by E.A.Jones, Boston

Concord in the Days of
Strawberries and Streetcars

The Milldam, July 1914. The trolley tracks were a sign of things to come. The horse and buggy were on their way out; the day of the automobile was about to begin. (Courtesy of the Concord Free Public Library)

1
A New Century Dawns

The arrival of a new century brought far greater changes to the lifestyle of the community than any that preceded it. Concord's population was less than five thousand; there was the comfortable and secure feeling of knowing one's neighbors; and the community looked to its own resources for recreation and amusement.

Open meadows and pasture land accompanied the many family farms that surrounded the residential village with its retail stores along the Milldam. A number of the buildings that existed then are readily identifiable today. The arrival of an industrial age was evident in the western part of town called Concord Junction, where small industries were concentrated and which existed in many ways as a separate community.

Laurence Richardson, a local historian, describes the sidewalks within Concord Center as "smooth gravel, wide enough for at least two to walk abreast. The trees were glorious, not yet interfered with by electric light wires and the laying of water and sewer pipes and street pavement. Some of the elms were so big they nearly blocked the sidewalk." House fences of wood or iron, he says, often had in front of them a six-to-eight-inch block of granite

that made stepping into a carriage easier, and there were hitching posts made either of wood or stone.

The horse and carriage, the bicycle, and the electric streetcar were the common means of transportation. A bad traffic situation might well have been caused by a herd of cows being driven along the road, for as Richardson records, there were 1,252 cows counted in Concord in 1900. On holidays and Sundays, he says, "the bicycle clubs from around Boston swarmed the roads in groups of 50 to 100. The riders, dressed in brightly colored striped jerseys which were as loud as their cries, rode noisily through the town. The one policeman on duty tried hard to control them and reported (in 1900) four arrests for speeding, that is, riding a bicycle over ten miles per hour."

It was a time for canoe outings and meadow picnics, the clanging of the trolley, the purchase of a five-cent block of ice from the iceman, the lamplighter making his rounds, the sound of the hurdy-gurdy, the local baseball games, dances, silent movies, and minstrel shows. Like many American small towns at the time, class lines were well defined. A census listing of occupations identified a servant class of "hired" men and women; and the 1900 census classified those of English background to be American, while listing other groups as ethnic nationalities.

Concord was regarded as a Yankee New England town, reflecting an Anglo dominance in economic, social, and political power, even as it was absorbing large

The home of Edwin Shepard Barrett on Liberty Street, called Battle Lawn. Men are at work haying, while others follow a more leisurely bent. Open meadow and pasture marked the Concord countryside. Circa 1900. (Collection of the Concord Historical Commission)

Main Street looking east with overarching elms. Hitching posts stand in front of the homes. Circa 1900. (Courtesy of the Concord Free Public Library)

numbers of the new arrivals from non-English backgrounds. Assimilation and the melting pot at work over succeeding generations have produced increasingly multi-ethnic backgrounds for many of us. That somehow Concord continues to be thought of as a Yankee community says something about the expansion of the term to now embrace a concept that extends beyond the strict definition of national origin.

Last Days of the Horse and Buggy

A really big event was hiring a horse and two-seated buggy for a Sunday afternoon drive, recalls Thomas Ryan. "My father and I sat in the front seat, my mother and two older sisters in the back seat. And the cost I learned later was two dollars."

There was a special or dress-up carriage for those Sunday rides, describes Gladys Clark, "kept neat and clean and covered during the week and kept in stables behind the homes of those that lived in town. The women who had maids would go out riding in the afternoons, and a few had coachmen. The ladies would sit in the back with their parasols, and I still have one of these. Even as the automobile came in,

there were people who held on to their horse and carriage."

Whitney Smith remembers both sets of his grandparents, the Smiths and the Blanchards, taking him in their horse and carriage around town. "We used to go on rides in the afternoon so that the ladies could get the air. Sometimes we would go around what they called the 'two mile square,' which was down Lowell Road to Barnes Hill Road to Monument Street and back. The longer ride, the 'five mile square,' was across Barrett's Mill Road into West Concord and down Main Street back into town again."

They were two Lexington Road neighbors on a Sunday morning in 1915. Ben Clark, whose family in Concord predates the American Revolution, leans on the double cane. Terence McHugh had emigrated from Ireland and purchased his farmhouse in 1880. (Collection of the Concord Historical Commission)

2

On the Milldam

The Milldam in Concord Center has retained a stable and discernible appearance over the years, and there is history in storefronts as they evolve and reflect the needs and times of the community. Sometimes it is the items sold that are recalled years later, but often it is the personality and style of the proprietor that has left a lasting impression.

"Going into town," for Gladys Clark, born in 1892, who lived a mile and a half up Lowell Road, "was like going to the circus for us farm folks. My first memory was of the depressing Middlesex Hotel which dominated the entrance to the town—a large, decrepit, brown building with a porch facing the Unitarian Church, where on the Fourth of July they had exhibits." As a young girl she remembers the streets being "just plain dirt country roads. There were hitching posts all along the street, and on Saturday all the farmers drove to town and hitched their horses there. Saturday afternoon was a big shopping time for the farmers."

The stores remained open late on Saturday evening till ten or eleven o'clock, says Sanfred Benson, born in 1897, and that was when he came in with his family from Ball's Hill Road. "Most farm people had only work horses, not driving horses and

you couldn't very well make a horse trot into town after a day's work during the week. Many people didn't reach town until 8:30 on a Saturday night."

Mark Mara, born in 1906, worked as a youth at the grocery store owned by his uncle, John Mara, who advertised as "the store with the smiling service." "I would groom the horses, bring the trash to Brister's Hill, where the dump was then, and at 7:00 A.M. grind fifty pounds of coffee, cut the lard and butter, weigh and price them and then start to fill out the orders. By nine o'clock I was on my route and back before noon to change and groom the horses. We got through usually at 10:00 P.M., Saturday nights at 11:00 P.M., and I got the big sum of ten dollars a week."

On the same side of the street as John Mara's grocery store was Towle and Kent, which later became Anderson's Market. Lars Anderson had worked for Towle and Kent, and Gladys Clark remembers him as "the man who came around taking the orders every Wednesday morning and delivering them at three in the afternoon. He was a wonderful salesman. If you ordered a yeast cake, he would always ask, 'and a barrel of flour?' "

Clark remembers Frank Pierce's shoe store, located next to Towle and Kent, as being on the Milldam from the Civil War era. "He was a dapper little man who was as neat as a pin and his store was the same way. You sat on a little bench that was covered with carpeting, and that's more than you got at any other shoe store. He

To the right of Mr. Whitcomb's was J.D.
Murray's grocery store. Circa 1900. (Courtesy
of the Concord Free Public Library)

8 On the Milldam

spent all the time in the world fitting your shoes just as if he were fitting a glove to your hand."

Next to Frank Pierce's store was a Chinese laundry. "The owner was a Christian oriental, very kind and friendly," says Clark. "He used to have nuts to give to the children and in the spring he would give us flower bulbs. I like to think of him as having a pigtail, but maybe its because I wish that he had one. His little shop was a busy place for there were plenty of businessmen and lawyers who went to Boston every day and had to dress up."

Across the street, where the Mary Curtis shop is now located, was the store owned by Mr. Whitcomb, whom Clark remembers as a very gracious elderly man. "That was the store that the children loved. He had a great case of drawers containing stock for all seasons, from tiny little dolls not more than two inches long up to seven or eight inches, and they varied in price from a penny a piece to ten cents. Another drawer would be filled with valentines, another with paper dolls, tops, marbles, and all kinds of candies like licorice dolls, and May baskets—you name it, he had it.

Vanderhoof's hardware store. Philip Moreau is on the left, and founder of the store in 1904, Albert Vanderhoof is on the right. Circa 1915. (Collection of the Concord Historical Commission, courtesy of Marguerite Moreau Melanson)

"And the prices were within reason. If you had five cents, you could always buy something to satisfy your heart. It didn't matter to him whether you bought one-cent worth and it took you a half hour to decide." Miss Houghton, who succeeded Mr. Whitcomb, had the same pleasing manner through the 1920s and early 1930s, relates David Little. The store was torn down, he adds, and replaced by a new building.

But the atmosphere changed, however, when Clark went next door to Billy Cross's dry goods store. His name she says, "suited him to a turn. He was a brisk little man bent on business. He had two clerks who never smiled, and they sat around that pot bellied stove. The whole atmosphere of that store was quite different. He carried everything from needles to underwear and yard goods. And if he didn't have it, he'd say, it wasn't manufactured anymore, and that was it."

It was not unusual for a local businessman to hold a town office and to carry out his duties right where he worked, and Cross was also the town clerk. Many long-time residents bought their hunting and fishing licenses from his store, and, adds Anna Manion, "marriage licenses and birth certificates were dispensed between sales of dry goods over the counter."

Mr. Urquhart's bakery, where Brigham's is now, is remembered by Mara for its outstanding pastries and bread. Clark explains that while most households did their own baking, there were items like

Veteran of the Milldam, Frank Pierce stands in front of his shoe store. Left to right: Lars Anderson, Charles Towle, Nathan Davis, Leslie Anderson, Charles Whitney, Frank Pierce, Daniel Potter, Michael Finigan, John Mara, Ernest Hinsman, and Ole O. Thorpe. Circa 1910. (Courtesy of the Concord Free Public Library)

The many drawers of Mr. Henry Whitcomb's store held affordable treasures that children could take their time looking through. Circa 1900. (Courtesy of the Concord Free Public Library)

éclairs, cream puffs, and fancy cakes that the housewife didn't make herself. She remembers him as one of the merchants who came around to people's houses filling orders. "The merchants always had the news and they were glad to impart it. And we would add our little five cents' worth too. Our butcher came around twice a week and you went out to the cart to choose what you wanted. It's a wonder that we aren't all down at Sleepy Hollow; I don't remember any ice on the cart and the same went for the fish man."

Nathan A. Davis's meat market, located next to Richardson's drugstore, is remembered by Mara as a great meat market. His son, Dr. William Davis, recalls that his father was an avid hunter who bought and sold a lot of local game which he hung at the entrance to the store. "He had quite a corps of men working for him. He used to go into Boston to get specialties and bring them out with him, and most of his time seemed to be spent on the railroad, on which he would leave as early as 6:00 A.M."

At the end of each day, the merchants used to go into Richardson's drugstore, says Gladys Clark, and Frank Pierce could be heard saying, " 'time to wood up, time to wood up,' and he would go over and put some more wood on the stove. Life among the merchants was very pleasant, gathering at the end of the day with their comments." Across from Richardson's was John Friend's drugstore, now Snow's Pharmacy, where the telephone company was located upstairs for a time. Longtime residents remark that you went to one or the other drugstore but not to both.

When Elizabeth Babcock as a girl would buy some ribbon at Miss Buck's store, where Sally Ann's Bake Shop is, she would envision its connection to Louisa May Alcott's day. "The Alcotts were so alive to me and we had been told that Miss Buck trimmed Miss Alcott's hats, that I used to wonder if she had had the first end of the ribbon I was buying."

Down Walden Street, where Cooley's is now, was the post office, says Mara, "with Mr. Fred Tower, the Republican Postmaster, and Mr. William Byron, the Democratic Postmaster, switching each time the tide changed in Washington. I delivered the mail quite often and every evening would go up to the railroad station and put the mailbag up on the big hook that the Flyer to Chicago would reach out and take going about eighty miles an hour."

Further down at Tuttle's Livery, the horses for the fire station across the street were kept. It was at Tuttle's Livery that Mara drove carriages as a spare hand. "They were carriages with the surrey on top with a team of horses, and we would get fifty cents to drive people around and maybe stop at the Colonial Inn and wait for them to have dinner. Many times we would drive over to Sudbury to the Wayside Inn and back. We would get a dollar for that and it would take the whole day. Alongside, down the alley way, there was a little building where they used to shear the horses and that is where we used

Nathan A. Davis's meat market featured a
wide variety of meat, game, and grocery specialties. (Courtesy of the Concord Free Public
Library)

Interior view of market. Left to right: Leo
Chisholm, Henry Joslin, N.A. Davis, Katie
Fiske, Charlie Davis. Circa 1900. (Courtesy of
the Concord Free Public Library)

to get our summer haircuts, a baldy we called it, from Clarence Tuttle."

When Marian Miller arrived in 1920, to live on Main Street, she remembers being introduced to all the storekeepers on the Milldam, whom she found to be "very chatty and personable." She received her social introduction to the community through a tea given for her by a family friend. "Everyone came properly dressed with white gloves and calling cards. They then called on me and I was obliged to return their calls." As market and meeting place over the years, the Milldam has stood at the heart of the town's center, the embodiment of its Main Street.

Charles Evans, Nick Macone, and Ed Donovan,
in front of John Keyes's bicycle shop on Walden
Street. Circa 1910. (Courtesy of the Concord
Free Public Library)

Post office staff about 1910. Left to right: Front row seated—special delivery boy Charles Edgarton, assistant postmaster Samuel Tuttle, postmaster Fred Tower, clerk Henry Murray. Standing—carriers William Dee, Henry Helsher, George Shepard, Patrick Cull. Third row—Thomas Mansfield, Joseph Swan. (Courtesy of the Concord Free Public Library)

Tuttle's Livery on Walden Street. Circa 1900.
(Courtesy of the Concord Free Public Library)

1930s view of the Milldam. (Courtesy of the
Concord Free Public Library)

19   On the Milldam

Concord volunteer firemen about 1912 at the central fire station on Walden Street with the town's first piece of motorized fire equipment, purchased in 1910. Left to right: Back row—Bert Lang, Denny Horne, unidentified fire fighter. Seated—Martin Finigan, Doc Holden, Jack Manning. Front row standing—Roy Bass, Bill Chisholm, Michael Finigan. Roy Bass was hired in 1914 as the first permanent fireman at a salary of $590 a year. "When I joined the fire department in 1935, we were really dependent on our call force, made up of men who lived and worked in the town and could respond when the fire whistle sounded." (From the memories of Thomas Tombeno, member of the Concord Fire Department, 1935–1974, and Fire Chief, 1959–1974. Photo courtesy of Ed Finigan)

Horse-drawn hook and ladder along the
Milldam. Turn of the century. (Courtesy of Robert MacLeod)

3
Your Neighborhood and Mine

Concord Junction

It was the concentration of railroad tracks that gave Concord Junction its name and contributed to the commercial life and development of this village community.

In 1872 the Framingham and Lowell, connecting with the Old Colony Railroad, built a line across the Fitchburg to create Concord Junction, explains Laurence Richardson. Four years later the Concord, New Hampshire, and Montreal, built the Acton, Nashua, and Boston through Dunstable, East Groton, Westford, and Acton to connect with the Fitchburg at Concord Junction. The New Haven trains that went from Lowell to Framingham to Fall River connected with the Fall River boat to New York and was a popular way to travel, says Florence Damon. "There was wonderful service on those trains."

As many as 125 trains a day passed through the Junction, says Edith Bailey. In addition to the regular passenger and freight trains, she remembers the high-speed trains, such as the Continental Limited and the Minuteman passing through, and the troop trains during war time. "At the time of World War I, my mother was among those offering the soldiers doughnuts and apples."

Her brother, Charlie Comeau, remembers his daily commute as a high school student from the Junction Depot, which he describes as a handsome, well-maintained facility. "We paid our own fare on the streetcar and when that stopped running in the early 1920s, we depended on the train."

Brick MacWilliams's father was a section boss for the railroad. "He always had a big crew that kept the trains and track in spic-and-span shape, and the grass area around it mowed. He kept his tools in the shacks visible in some of the old pictures of the station. They had in those days an interlocking tower that set the signals for the express trains to go through and did the switching for the freight trains. Out in back of the tower was a turntable that was used to turn engines around so they could reverse direction without backing up. As kids we used to get a kick out of watching those engines turn around."

And going to West Concord in the earlier days of this century, remarks Richardson, was almost like going to another community. Forty years before 1900, he adds, there was no Concord Junction. "The Derby farmhouse and barns (where the shopping center is now) were nearly alone across from the fire station. Near the outlet of Warner's Pond were the few buildings of the Lead Works; and a mile

The Continental Limited approaching Concord
Junction station. Circa 1915. (Collection of the
Concord Historical Commission)

Commonwealth Avenue, the heart of the Junction. Circa 1915 (Collection of the Concord Historical Commission)

farther out Main Street, where it crosses the Assabet, were a few houses around the Damon Cotton Factory. This changed as Concord Junction grew by the addition of its railroad employees."

"To live in West Concord," relates Elsie Kennedy, "was to live in the industrial end of town and you were aware of that distinction growing up." The separation was a physical one as well, since there were few homes then along Main Street that linked both sections of town. It was the high school, she observes, that brought the young people from both ends of town together, though she resented having to pay the electric streetcar fare to get there every day.

A vote of Town Meeting in 1928 changed the name of Concord Junction to West Concord, and Maude Ellis, who came to Concord in 1921, remembers the controversy. "My husband was the secretary of the Chamber of Commerce at the time there was a wish to change the name and it was rather controversial because many people wanted to keep the Junction name. The Chamber of Commerce was quite influential in getting the name changed and we were very pleased with this, because being outsiders, we could see there was a noticeable feeling between the two parts of town."

Comeau describes the West Concord of his youth as made up of hardworking church-going people with very few diversions other than baseball and family gatherings. "There were a great many poor people, really poor. I recall people picking

Brick MacWilliams. 1983. (Photo by Alice Moulton)

up the trimmings and bark from the Allen Chair Company to heat their homes. Often boys would go up and down the railroad tracks to pick up the lumps of coal that had fallen down. Most of the boys worked at that time and it was a common thing at eleven or twelve years of age. My father owned the farm and the contracting business, so I never had the chance to be a juvenile delinquent."

For Bailey, born on Commonwealth Avenue in 1902, a step back to the first three decades of this century is an easy walk to take, as she brings back the commercial life of the heart of the Junction. It was commonplace for an owner of a store to live with his family in the back or above his business. The stores offered basic services, but it was the presence of manufacturing that distinguished West Concord from its counterpart in Concord Center. Ever present also in Bailey's reminiscences is the destruction caused by fire.

By the time Bailey was born, Warner's Pail Factory had ceased manufacturing and was practically a ruin. The bridge along Commonwealth Avenue, where it was located, serves as a convenient starting point for her narrative. Opposite the Pail Factory had been a canning factory, which became a laundry and later burned. Purchased by Dan Hayes, it was converted to the Concord Garnett Mill, which processed recycled wool and is the present site of the Leather Shop.

A great open space was followed by a long building extending from Common-

---

The Damon Mill had become the Strathmore Worsted Mills when Brick MacWilliams worked there in 1918. "It was fascinating to go into the basement to see all the machinery that ran the mill and on the upper floors the spinning machines and the skill that it took to run those. A number of the workers came from Belgium and spoke French." Circa 1900. (Collection of the Concord Historical Commission)

Edith Bailey. 1978. (Photo by Alice Moulton)

Charlie Comeau. 1978. (Photo by Alice Moulton)

Workers of the Boston Harness Company located on Main Street by the bridge over the Assabet River. The company was founded by Harvey Wheeler in 1890. Circa 1900. (Collection of the Concord Historical Commission)

wealth Avenue back towards the river. It housed a general store owned by Loring Fowler in the front and, attached to it, was a livery stable with a blacksmith in the back. This too was totally destroyed by fire one night. Bailey was born in the double house, now an upholstery company, which was originally a barn built for the blueine company though never used. Where the West Concord Five & Ten is now was the Bartolomeo block owned by Sal Bartolomeo, who ran a large fruit store and lived with his family in the back. On the second floor was Harry Fritz, the tailor, who also used the rear of the store for his family's living quarters.

A dry goods store, where the auto parts shop is, was owned by Messrs. London and Erdang and was like a department store, where Bailey says she worked when in high school. The building next to this was the Association Hall, which burned in September 1903 and was rebuilt. She connects this fire with family stories about John Fitzgerald, the father of Rose Kennedy and later mayor of Boston, who lived for a time in West Concord along Main Street. "He was a politician who used to chase fires. My father had a lot of stories to tell about that. John Fitzgerald always went to all the fires around and got into difficulty with the firemen. He and the local fire chief definitely didn't get on."

The Association Hall building was rebuilt to include the present post office. Also included on the first floor was the Rexall Store, run by C. Hayden Whitney.

The Association Hall, which Bailey describes as the mainstay of the social life for the West Concord community, was on the second story. "Association Hall was where we saw movies, attended dances and minstrel shows. That was the whole core of our

Postman Bert Bass delivers the mail along Commonwealth Avenue. The blueine company did such a large mail-order business that it elevated West Concord to a higher grade post office than Concord Center, and its postal carriers wore uniforms. Circa 1912. (Collection of the Concord Historical Commission, courtesy of Jim Condon)

social life." On the third floor was the Odd Fellows Hall, which was used for all the local fraternal organizations. Today the upper two stories no longer exist.

The thriving blueine factory started by George Conant was set back on Beharrell Street where the printing company is now. The blueine solution was used at this time for the family wash, and a brisk mail order business made it possible for many young people to find part-time work there. Ads were placed regularly on the Sunday comic pages offering prize incentives for school children selling the blueine for ten cents a package. The volume of business done elevated West Concord to a higher class post office than Concord Center. Concord Junction had uniformed letter carriers, adds Richardson, that were seldom found outside a city.

On the other side of Commonwealth Avenue, across the street from the former Pail Factory, was the small town square. The house on the corner of Bradford Street and Commonwealth Avenue was built for the Whitney family, says Bailey, "and that is where I used to push General Otis Whitney around in his baby carriage." To the rear was the Allen Chair Company, now Bradford Furniture, which Bailey estimates must have been built about 1908, from playing there as a child while it was being constructed. Where the hardware store is now was a bicycle shop whose owners lived above the store; and next to it, the Elmwood Hotel which has since been remodeled into apartments. Alongside was Adams and Bridges grocery store and the

Hay shoe store, which is still at the addition that Loring Fowler built when his general store across the street burned. For a time Robert Carter, Sr., had his furniture store there, she adds, before he built the current building on Main Street.

Bailey can continue along Main Street, bringing back once again a boarding house, luncheonette, small grocery store, ice cream parlor, and barber shop. She remembers when the Harvey Wheeler School was being built in 1918 and her father, Edward A. Comeau, was given the task of moving the nearby livery stable across the railroad tracks to Commonwealth Avenue. Comeau, who ran a stonemason and construction business, chose Palm Sunday as a quiet day, with far fewer trains to cope with, and successfully moved the livery on wooden rollers to the site where the Edwardsen and Soberg Mobil Station is located. The three-story building which housed the barbershop belonging to Mike Kelley and the ice cream parlor of Charlie Hogan, says Bailey, was totally destroyed by fire on 17 March 1932. It is a fire that stands out in her memory for it originated in the fire station itself, where the Village Cleaners now stands, and the firefighters from Acton were the first to come to the rescue.

Employees of the Allen Chair Company gather in front of the building that has become Bradford Furniture, mid 1930s. (Courtesy of Bradford Furniture)

31　Your Neighborhood and Mine

The snow falls gently around John Mandrioli as he stands in front of the West Concord Fruit Store shortly after the business moved to its present Commonwealth Avenue location in 1936. Mandrioli, an immigrant from Bologna, Italy, had originally opened a fruit store in 1919 at the corner of Main Street and Commonwealth Avenue, where it was affectionately known as "John Bananas." (Courtesy of Peter Mandrioli)

Reformatory Circle

The prison today is an alien institution within Concord. Renewed community anger and irritation accompanies each local prison outbreak, while public skepticism greets prison official assurances that improved security measures are being undertaken. Regarded as anything but an integral part of the community, the mention of its possible expansion brings forth immediate resistance. There are town residents, though, who remember when living near the prison brought no fear and when the reformatory provided a source of jobs.

The story of Concord's correctional institution begins in 1873 when the state of Massachusetts found it necessary to build a prison to replace the one at Charlestown which was considered inadequate. The state legislature appropriated $1 million to find a site and build the prison and since land prices in Concord were significantly lower than near Boston, the Cook Farm was purchased along with some adjoining property and the work started in the spring of 1873.

The new state penitentiary opened in 1878 with 700 inmates from Charlestown and the staff occupied the row of white houses on Commonwealth Avenue. Laurence Richardson describes in his writings the interest of local citizens in the prison inmates and officers. "Weekly in the newspaper the townspeople were offered every bit of prison news and gossip, including biographical details of each new arrival, his offense, and the length of his sentence. General Chamberlin, the superintendent, brought his family, and the ladies of Concord rushed to make formal

The Concord Reformatory. Circa 1900. (Courtesy of the Concord Free Public Library)

33   Your Neighborhood and Mine

Concord Reformatory staff and officers. 1918. Left to right: Seated: Fred Lawton, Charles Wales, Superintendent Percy Allen, Charles Judge, Fred Reed, George Hagerty, George Blake, Richard McSweeny. Standing, first row, and immediately in back: Tom Blood, unidentified, John Allen, David Ball, Jim Hennessy, Joe Doherty, William Fitzgerald, unidentified, Charlie Sheehan, Stuart Farquhar, John Bowen, Albert Shaw, unidentified, Patrick

Prendergast, John Anderson, William Logan,
Leon Harris, John Clement. Standing, back
row: Frank Walker, Ralph Whidden, Fred
Hewitt, Harold Judkins, John Hannon, John
Mitchell, Neal O'Connell, Fred Taylor, John

McCleary, Louis McCaffrey, Martin Gilligan,
Anson Hix, Tom Frawley, unidentified, John
Connorton, George Hodgon. (Courtesy of Mary
Connorton)

calls on his wife and daughters. Twice a day barges ran from the Middlesex Hotel in Concord Center and people with boats rowed up the Assabet River on Sundays to picnic on the grounds."

The Middlesex Central railroad extended its service to the prison in 1879, where a turntable and an engine house were built, as well as a station building with a restaurant and hotel on the upper floors. The Middlesex Central was later taken over by the Boston and Lowell, which in turn combined with the Boston and Maine Railroad. Marguerite Leighton's father was a conductor on the southern division of the Boston and Maine Railroad, which ran from Boston to the reformatory station. She describes the run as "a very popular line and patronized by many. As a child one of my happy recollections was to ride as the train backed out and the engine disconnected and put on the turntable before going into the old brick roundhouse. We always felt badly to see this old landmark disappear."

Elsie Kennedy remembers the round house and turnaround area as being located where the State Police barracks now stand. The reformatory station building was later torn down to make way for the rotary junction of Routes 2 and 2A. Kennedy, born in 1904, grew up along Barrett's Mill Road and her father was a pig farmer for the reformatory. "They raised the meat for many of the state institutions. It was really very interesting. When there was a new family of piglets,

the children in my family went down with my dad to see them. At that time the working part of the reformatory was known as the old stockade and there were cow barns, the pig area, and the large stable of horses used for farming and driving. There was a lot of pride and interest in the work that the men did at that time.

"Concordians took for granted having the reformatory and its inmates in the area. It had always been there. If there were an escape, we were totally unconcerned. So we had no fear of having it here. And the men that worked there definitely played a part with their families in contributing to the life in West Concord." Today she is troubled by the lack of care of the physical facilities of the prison and the homes of employees. "The grounds used to be eye-catching, beautifully cared for, the houses were kept in good repair. Today I feel the state owned houses are really no credit to the community."

"The reformatory officers at that time were among the most respected people in town," recalls Florence Damon. "Some of the biggest homes on Commonwealth Avenue and Main Street belonged to the reformatory officers. Reformatory workers could rent the big Victorian duplex houses known as the white row of homes on Commonwealth Avenue for twelve dollars a month, with the heat furnished by steam pipes from the reformatory itself. In addition, reformatory workers also lived in a green row of houses on what was known as Elm Place."

Damon, a longtime member of the West Concord Women's Club, explains that her club was founded in 1902 by the wives of three reformatory officers, and the members met on the third floor of the old Association Hall. "They wanted to promote educational, philanthropic, and social needs and seemed to devote a great deal of time to reading Ruskin."

The reformatory, says Charlie Comeau, had a great influence over West Concord, and the people who worked there were a little better paid than the average person. The prison operated a variety of industries which included the manufacture of furniture, hats, clothing, and harness making. The inmates were employed by local contractors, a practice which encouraged related industries to operate outside the prison. There were also evening courses in the academic subjects. The instructors were recruited from among the young men of the area as well as college students who needed employment to pay for their education.

Thomas Ryan's father worked at the reformatory as an instructor for $1,000 a year. The officers who manned the towers, the walls, and the high benches overlooking each work room, he says, earned $1,200. "These jobs were among the highest paying in town, particularly at a time when factory workers were making ten to fifteen dollars for a fifty-five hour work week."

During his early high school days, while working for Mr. Young's meat market,

Ryan's duties included filling the orders sent in by reformatory inmates, most of which he says were for cookies, candies, and fruits that were delivered each Thursday evening. At the end of his senior year in high school, he and his friend, John Garvey, were asked by Dick McSweeney, an officer at the reformatory who had taken an interest in them, if they would like a job teaching night school at two dollars per night twice a week. "I could hardly believe it and accepted at once. There were four school nights, and six classes each of fifty to sixty prisoners. There was no attempt at classification, so that each class was composed of illiterates up to high school graduates, eighteen to fifty years old."

Night school, he said, started at 6:15 P.M. and ended by a gong at 8:15 P.M. "During those two hours each teacher was on his own. I was the youngest teacher, the others were regular officers or instructors who wanted to supplement their salaries, now called moonlighting. Discipline was absolutely strict. The prisoners knew that on the front of the teacher's desk was a button to be pressed in case of any trouble, which immediately brought in an officer who took charge. He hustled out of the room any prisoner who caused trouble. They all knew this meant solitary confinement and a blot on their record. Also they would be denied the privilege of going to night school for a period of time, and spent the time behind the dreaded bars of their cells.

"During the five years I taught, I had occasion only once to push the button. A big surly prisoner in the back row had thrown a blackboard eraser at my head. I was lucky to have ducked in time and pushed the button. I never saw that prisoner again." The teaching experience was deemed a worthwhile one and Ryan added that his friend, John Garvey, after graduating from Harvard took on "the idealistic but frustrating job" as Superintendent of Schools at the reformatory. Harold Chase also taught evening classes and noted that inmates were graded and allowed certain privileges according to their grade level. "It was a model reformatory attracting many visitors."

On Sundays many townspeople went to church there and commended the work of prison chaplains like the Reverend William Batt in helping to form the West Concord Union Church in 1893. Robert Carter's father played the church organ at the prison from 1918 through 1935 and once a week would rehearse the inmate choir. The organ in those days had to be hand-pumped by the inmates and Carter remembers one inmate urging his father " 'not to play too hard.' He had a good relationship with the prisoners. My father told the story of meeting a man in Boston whom he didn't recognize and the man reminded him. 'Don't you remember? I was at the big house in Concord.' "

"A lot of speakers would come to the prison and many of the people around would attend," says Carter's mother, Winifred. "I used to have a lot of company in those days and I would take all my visitors to services there on Sunday mornings." Before moving to Highland Street, where he was born in 1922, Robert Carter's parents lived across from the reformatory where the gas station is located at the rotary. Winifred Carter describes the prisoners as good neighbors. "If I was washing windows on the outside and dropped my cloth and prisoners were walking by to the farm, they would pick it up and bring it to me. The same was true if I had wash on the line and it would blow away. We didn't fear them at all."

Up Lowell Road, Along the Plain

A mile out of the center of town, no matter which direction you turned, you were surrounded by farm folk, says Gladys Clark. In the late 1800s and early 1900s, she explains, different sections of town were recognized by distinctive names. And at the intersection of Barrett's Mill and Lowell roads was the self-contained community of Hildreth's Corner, which had an identity of its own.

"I think perhaps it started when Mr. Hildreth built the big brick house at the corner where Lowell and Barrett's Mill Road intersect. Directly behind that house, he built a store which had everything that this area needed from molasses and vinegar, right through to spools of thread and

Gladys Clark. 1978. (Photo by Alice Moulton)

underwear. It was a wonderful gathering place in the evenings, especially for the men in the community. In the winter they gathered there to play checkers and I have the checker board that belonged to my grandfather.

"Next door was a little cobbler shop, and alongside that a blacksmith shop. When I was a child the store and the cobbler shop were gone, but the blacksmith's shop owned by McClellan, a hard-boiled Scotsman, was still there. Everybody in this area took their horses there to have them shod. There was also a little cooper's shop and I suppose by having the sawmill there on Barrett's Mill Road, there would be lumber for the barrels which would be

used for apples. The grist mill, alongside the saw mill, was where the corn was taken. It was a pretty lively little mill until about 1917–1918, when people began buying their grain at a store instead of raising corn for their own grain." And Clark adds that a look at the store ledgers at that time show that people bought just what they needed and could afford.

"The stretch of family farms that extended from Hildreth Corner to 'the lane,' now called Hugh Cargill Road, was open and level and known as 'the plain.' My house was the last one on the plain. The farms were well maintained and productive and most were occupied by the second or third generations with the furnishings and atmosphere of comfortable living. Cows supplied the home with all the milk necessary. Cottage cheese was made from the surplus milk, especially in the summer when the milk didn't keep very well, but butter was no longer made at home because of the length of time required." A man under contract would come around each day to pick up and take the milk to Cambridge, where it was processed for distribution to Boston and surrounding communities. This was similiar to the daily collection of strawberries and asparagus to Boston's Faneuil Hall for the produce merchants.

"I think back now to all the hard work that went into raising these strawberries and asparagus and if we got twelve cents a box for strawberries, and twenty-five cents for two to three bunches of asparagus, we

The saw and grist mills of Barrett's Mill Road,
part of the Hildreth Corner community. Circa
1900. (Courtesy of the Concord Free Public
Library)

thought we were doing very well. So farming was not a profitable career by any means. Those who raised corn for market sent their crop in the fall to Boston, while potatoes were raised for home use, along with vegetables like carrots and turnips that were put in the root cellar for winter's use. Of course everybody had their chickens and eggs. Although we didn't have any, there were always people who raised pigs, and in the fall they would slaughter some of these and we would buy pork and salt pork, which was put down in kegs for the winter. One thing we had on our farm was Indian corn, which we raised and took to the grist mill to be ground for corn meal, our very own corn meal right from the farm to the mill to our cupboards to our tummies. And of course there were also apples that were made into sweet cider, and if it turned a little too soon, which it sometimes did, that was our vinegar."

Wood was the main source of fuel and there was always the woodlot, she says, "to keep people busy and out of mischief." "In those days there was some wonderful lumber in the woods. The telephone company was always looking for the chestnut trees for the telephone poles, and when my father built our barn, he went into the woods and chose some chestnut trees for the great underpinnings of the barn and when it burned, those chestnut underpinnings didn't, they just stayed solid. As children, we just couldn't wait for the first heavy frost in the fall to run off in the woods to see the chestnuts that had fallen

during the night. The burrs are on the trees until the frost comes and opens them and the chestnuts drop to the ground. Then it was a scramble whether the squirrels, chipmunks, or we kids would get the nuts. The elms were a mark of beauty, the oak was used for lumber in many local buildings, and the willow trees at the time of World War I were used for the powder mills. I can still see a team of four horses taking those big trunks of trees to the sawmill."

Clark recalls the abundant vineyards, apple and pear orchards, that her grandfather planted in the mid-nineteenth century on land that he owned "up the lane," experimenting with different varieties. "Farmer's Cliff Road is named after Jacob Farmer, whose farm my grandfather had bought. When my brother found that he could no longer continue farming here, he sold the land into house lots and the street that was put on it was called Farmer's Cliff Road because if you go to the end of the road, you will see a cliff. At one time there was a soap factory up the lane also. As a child I can remember seeing sort of a wall built up and two big iron kettles. That is something in history that was never recorded. People just knew about it and forgot it."

So many of the earlier houses on Lowell Road have disappeared as well, explains Clark, often from fire. "All along Lowell Road there were these lovely old houses built four square right next to the road and belonged to the Dakin, Davis, and

Melvin families, who seemed to intermarry. Then the people on Estabrook Road, like my family, the Clarks, married the Balls and the Flints."

While the men of the household were engaged in farm work or their trades, life for the women centered around the home. "They provided three hearty meals a day that began with breakfast at six o'clock, for every farm had cows where the milk had to be ready for delivery by then. Monday and Tuesday were usually the days that were set aside for washing and ironing, done by hand. The laundry was a major chore that required the black iron on the kitchen stove. Often the washing and ironing meant the hiring of extra help when affordable. With the midweek being used as catch up days and cleaning done on Friday, Saturday was the big baking day.

"And what a day that was. Beans that had to be baked were soaked overnight, sculled, and put into the pot the first thing Saturday morning with a goodly piece of salt pork, mustard, and molasses with water added to cover. Into the oven went the pot for a day of baking. Then came the pie making, several of them—apple, rhubarb, blueberry, squash, mince, or lemon, as the season dictated. Next came pudding or cake, and then the brown bread was steamed for the afternoon. And when the white bread which had been mixed the night before was ready, it was put into the pans to rise and bake. Never can one forget the nostalgic odors of a Saturday afternoon in the kitchen, the freshly washed wooden floor, and all the fragrances of the baking and beans. Sunday was the well-earned day of rest and with the main meal already prepared the day before, this was a time for social visits from friends, especially during the summer when travel was not a problem.

"The women of the neighborhood, about ten or twelve of them would meet in the afternoon, once or twice a month, to sew while one member read from a recent book. No refreshments, not even tea, were served. No doubt the hearty noon meal and the need to prepare another for the six o'clock supper stirred no desire for a victual." The young women of the plain, says Clark, if they did not marry, were likely to become teachers or pursue art or music. And there always seemed to be a plentiful number of girls around "caring for their families." Concord, laughs Clark, seemed noted for its monuments and old maids.

Life Back of the Depot

The depot area on Thoreau Street provided the commercial bustle for Concord Center the way the Junction did for West Concord. At the depot the Fitchburg division of the Boston & Maine carried its passengers, the freight trains their produce, with cars transporting cattle and horses. Mailbags were tossed out and new ones picked up; it seemed all in an instant as the train sped by.

The streets behind the depot became a distinct neighborhood center and the surrounding neighborhoods of Hubbardville and Herringville shared in and

The Fitchburg division of the Boston and
Maine Railroad passes at Belknap Street. 1900.
(Courtesy of the Concord Free Public Library)

depended on the commerce of the district. Jim Powers grew up on Grant Street. "Back of the depot" included, he says, Belknap Street (then called High Street), Grant, Brooks, Elsinore, and Byron streets, and a portion of Sudbury Road. "It was a neighborhood that was primarily Irish, with a large group of Italians and quite a few Norwegians and Swedes. They all mixed together, and it was a nice, big happy family back there."

His father was a gate or crossing tender in his later years, at the railroad station, manually operating the gates. "Many times I had to pinch hit for my father, and I would tend crossing as a young fellow." He remembers the way the mail arrived and was picked up from the trains. "The trains would fly through. One of them, the Minuteman, was Concord's pride and joy, and was so called because its schedule called for a mile a minute. It came through Concord in late afternoon, and as it went through, the man on the baggage car would have the door open and the mailbag for Concord sitting on the edge of the door. And just as he got by the crossing, he would kick the bag out and it would go flying across the field. Then he immediately pulled a steel arm up that stuck out from the car and ahead of him would be a mailbag that was tied in the middle, and this arm on the car would snag that bag off its moorings and off it went at a mile a minute."

On Cottage Lane there was an area with a small group of houses that was called

Jim Powers. 1981. (Photo by Alice Moulton)

"the patch." "Along one of the railroad sidings, there were some holding pens for cattle, and I can remember them being driven down from Nine Acre Corner up Grant Street, across the tracks over to the holding pens of Cottage Lane. Usually there would be one or two cattle cars standing on the siding and they would load the cattle into the cars."

On Grant Street was a blacksmith shop owned by Tom McGann that Powers always felt was out of a picture postcard. "It was swayed back, it was so old, and partially caved in, and out on one side was a big mound of discarded horseshoes." Down the street on Sudbury Road, where the entrance to Stop and Shop is now, was another blacksmith's shop owned by Johnny

Moreau and his father Gus, and that, says Powers, was "neat as a pin." Out in front there was a great big circular granite rock on which they put the iron tires on the wheels. "It was quite an operation."

Horseshoes was one of the popular sports for the older men. "They would play every evening, two men to a team. They played from early spring until late fall, when they would light bonfires behind the stakes so they could see what they were pitching at. They took it quite seriously, and they were real horseshoes that they were pitching."

Herb Neeley had a big paint shop in the blacksmith's yard which is now Wilson Lumber. "He was truly an artist who would paint these carriages very fancy with little pinstripes. Down beneath he had stored a fantastic collection of beautiful carriages in which we played hide and seek." In the blacksmith's yard there was also a barn where Daiglan Curran had a couple of pigs and cows and where a lot of the neighbors, including Powers's family, bought their milk. "He milked the cows right there and poured the milk into these big containers and then into your quart or two-quart can. We bought milk every evening, it wasn't pasteurized, but it was really fresh milk."

Powers and his friends used to play baseball in the cattle show field at the end of Belknap and Elsinore streets. "It had once been the cattle show grounds, and the circus used to come there, even Barnum and Bailey. I can remember the circus trains being put on sidings there down by Wilson Lumber, and all the elephants early in the morning being marched up Belknap Street to the cattle show grounds where the tents were pitched. It was a very active place, and prior to that there was a half-mile race track up there, sulky racing they called it."

And with pocket money in hand, Powers and his friends would go over to Johnny Bart's fruit store across from the railway station where the Concord Package Store is now. "He had penny candy and ice cream and was quite a local character." Bartolomeo's fruit store was one of four stores that served the residents of the area. The others were Cutler's Grocery, Byron's Grocery, and Whitney's Meat Market.

Charlie Byron remembers well the grocery store that his father ran on Thoreau Street. "Coffee came unground and tea was according to type, such as oolong. People would want a quarter of a pound of this or that and we would bag it up. I can remember helping my father grind coffee. I was so small that I would have to stand on a wooden box to take the wheel around. Each store had its own route in each section of town. We would pick up molasses jugs, kerosene cans, and vinaigrette bottles that had woven rattan around them and then return them to the customers the next day filled."

Byron was born on Willow Street and moved with his family to Hubbard Street, where he still lives. It was then part of the

Gus Moreau's blacksmith shop on Sudbury
Road. 1895. (Courtesy of the Concord Free Public Library)

Charlie Byron. 1980. (Photo by Alice Moulton)

neighborhood known as Herringville, because of its many Nova Scotian residents. His daily routine as a young boy included going down to the barn on Thoreau Street to feed the two horses, harness, and hitch the team to be taken to his family's house, where his father would then bring them to the store. "We depended on horses for so much and had a little different feeling for animals in those days."

People delivering goods from Boston or Waltham, says Byron, would unhitch their horses and get fresh ones at McManus's livery stable on the corner of Middle Street to go as far as Littleton or Groton and would pick up their own horses on the way back. Ralph Hemenway adds that this was the time of horse-drawn fire engines, and

the horses for the firehouse were kept at McManus's stable. The livery also ran hacks or taxis for the people arriving on the train who needed transportation home and rented carriages for people who wanted tours of Concord. Hemenway laughs when he remembers a friend of his walking along Sudbury Road, where a tour had stopped in front of the house where the famous sculptor, Daniel Chester French, had worked on his models. The driver was heard to say, "this was the building where Daniel French scalped."

Hemenway was born on Fairhaven Road, at the foot of Potter Street, in the neighborhood called Hubbardville, named for the estate of Ebenezer Hubbard and the Hubbards who lived on Sudbury Road where Whittemore Street is now. Gertrude Hagerty, born in the same neighborhood, says her house on Whittemore Street was where George Hubbard's bountiful asparagus fields once were. Her sister Gladys Cull recalls the old lamplighter, Johnny Hansen, who had a shoe store on Walden Street, coming to Potter Street at Sudbury Road to light the lamp.

Anna Manion learned from the title of the family's old house on Fairhaven Road that most of the land was owned by Potters and Wheelers. Manion has lived on Fairhaven Road all her life. "I was born in the house next door at 12 Fairhaven Road where my father was born in 1870. My grandfather, Timothy Goulding, bought a house, barn, and three acres of land at the corner of Sudbury and Fairhaven roads in

Anna Manion. 1980. (Photo by Alice Moulton)

1869 for $1,100. The Wilfred Wheelers and the George Wheelers lived across from us, the Hemenways were up the street, and there were many Hagertys in the neighborhood.

"One mile from the center of town in Hubbardville and we were considered as living in the sticks," laughs Manion. Whether helping out picking strawberries, bunching asparagus, or filling her milk pail from a neighbor's cow, she looks back at a life that seemed uncomplicated and stable then. "One of my fondest memories is when my father gathered the hay from our field once a year to put in the haymow to feed the horse. We all helped pitch the hay onto the wagon and then we were lifted up on top to ride down to Belknap Street where the horse was kept."

Manion reflects that neighbors were good to each other and relied on each other. "Some of my dearest friends are the people I grew up with in this neighborhood. There was a sense of security by the permanence of the people and values. And these friends seem to have stayed nearby and have meant a great deal to me over the years. They were a fine basis from which to build a life."

On Fairhaven Hill

Life on Fairhaven Hill during the time of horses and sleighs was a golden time, remembers Helen Thompson, who lived high on its summit. "We all regretted very much when automobiles came in, convenient as they were.

"The pond was nice and big, we cut ice and the children skated there. Many Concord people owned woodlots around the lower part of the hill. In the dead of winter, when the snow was deep, Anderson's grocery store would deliver to the foot of the hill. The Norwegian nurse we hired would take the three boys down in a toboggan to get the groceries."

Vineyards were plentiful over most of the hill, but it was far too rocky for growing the asparagus that did so well elsewhere in town, Thompson explains. "Some of the men that we hired to plow broke their plows up here because of the rocks and refused to do it any more." She and

Helen Thompson. 1978. (Photo by Alice Moulton)

her husband Henry cultivated and successfully raised a bountiful supply of peaches from as many as 200 peach trees. "We had every kind of peach and sold them. We were advised not to have apple trees growing alongside the peach trees because the insects from the apple trees would infect them. So we hewed down the apple trees and depended on the peaches.

"We had something like twenty-nine rows of grapes. There was competition with the New York grape-growers at that time and it was difficult shipping the fruit around or out of the state. But I found a place near where the Antiquarian Museum is now and set up a stand to sell them. Any guest that we had in the house

was put to work lining straw boxes with leaves for the grapes to be sold. I had to get a license because one day the police came along and asked if I had one, which had never occurred to me. My husband never sold by the roadside, so he was perfectly glad that I was willing to do it."

Mary Abbott, who lived on Sudbury Road, loved the freedom that the pre-automobile era offered her to ride horseback. "I used to ride a great deal in Fairhaven woods. Before Route 2 was built I would just traverse a short piece of Sudbury Road to get to the woods. Many of these wood roads were cleared by my grandfather's woodsmen which made for beautiful riding. Riding in the winter with snow on the ground used to be wonderful because the roads would be opened by a team of horses so that you could go for miles on the hard packed snow, and if you were riding in company, you could go side by side."

The woods between Old Concord Road in Lincoln and Sudbury Road in Concord were largely owned by members of her family. "My grandfather, Charles Francis Adams II, who came to Lincoln in 1893, was the son of Charles Francis Adams, who was the ambassador to the Court of St. James's during the Civil War. There was much historical awareness in my family with two presidents and an ambassador. My grandfather's house overlooked Fairhaven Bay. He had a large parcel of woodland, and also rented land, on a ninety-nine year lease from the Boston and Maine Railroad on what used to be the

50   Your Neighborhood and Mine

old fairgrounds opposite Walden Pond. I remember his great distress in trying to control the gypsy moths in 1948. He tried extensive spraying, but had to give it up, the gypsy moths got the better of him. His nephew, Charles Francis Adams, built a house on Fairhaven Hill that has a white portico and is very visible from across the river on Sudbury Road. This joined my grandfather's land and my father also owned some land there."

Fairhaven Hill and the surrounding woods were an extension of the neighborhood for Anna Manion living on Fairhaven Road, in the days before Route 2. "We were allowed free rein of the woods surrounding Fairhaven Hill by the Thompson and Adams families. After school and on weekends, we would go up to Fairhaven Hill and coast down in front of the Adams house to the river. The pond at Arena farm was much bigger before Route 2 was built and we used to skate there. At night the boys would build fires and then we would go to somebody's house for hot chocolate. There seemed to always be piles and piles of snow and lots of ice when I was young. I remember the Adams daughter, Kathryn, riding past our house in her pony cart and then how excited we were to watch her wedding party when she married Harry Morgan of New York City, J. Pierpont Morgan's son. What a thrill!"

And while it was usually all very neighborly, Thompson remembers the time when she balked at a request from Mrs. Adams. "She asked to borrow my large silver coffee urn, which I loaned to her on other occasions. But when she told me it was for an anti-suffrage party, I told her she couldn't have it for I was decidedly in the other camp!"

View from the cliffs of Fairhaven Hill. Circa 1900. (Courtesy of the Concord Free Public Library)

4

When We Were a Couple of Kids

Of Winters Past

The snowdrifts seemed deeper and the bite of winter stronger in childhood memory when the landscape was less populated and the automobile only an occasional conveyance.

"During the winter when we were young," says Gertrude Hagerty, "we would get up and rush down to the potbellied stove to get dressed. We would hear the hounds barking and rush to the window to see the hunt go by. When the milk was delivered, the cream would be standing way up above the bottles. They used a horse blanket to cover the milk in the delivery pung to keep it from freezing, but that didn't do the trick."

"We always wore long underwear in the winter, down to the wrists and ankles," remembers Anna Manion. "Most of the houses had coal or wood stoves. We would jump out of bed in a freezing cold room, race downstairs to one of the fires below, get dressed, eat quickly, and go outside in the cold to school or play. We were living before furnaces, telephones, automobiles, or electricity were in general use."

When Velina Bregoli arrived in Concord, seventy years ago at age three, with her mother from Bologna, Italy, she had never seen snow before and resisted the efforts of the train conductor to put her down "in all that white stuff. My father had come earlier, and we lived on Belknap Street at the end of what was called Brennan's Block. Growing up, the winters seemed to me very severe. I don't remember snowplows when I was a little girl; the town had horse-drawn pungs that went over the snow, and we used to hop on to go off to school in those.

"Coming from a poor family we had very little, and I wanted a sled so badly. But my father said there just wasn't the money for it. One day though, he came to me and said, 'well, here's your sled,' and showed me what he had made out of beef ribs that he had brought home from the butcher's. I was so embarrassed by the sight, I wanted nothing to do with it. On Sundays we always went down to Nashawtuc Road because the river overflowed and there was always skating there below the hill. Well, there my father went down the hill with that sled. I stayed way behind, I didn't want anyone to know that he was even my father. But then I looked down and saw him sitting on his sled having a ball, and with all these skaters hanging on to him. What a wonderful sight that was!"

Nashawtuc Hill was nicknamed Nashawtuc Hell by some local mothers, recalls Helen Shaw. Before the decade of the

---

Public transportation on the barge. Circa 1900. (Courtesy of the Concord Free Public Library)

sixties, when it was given to the town as conservation land, the popular sledding slope belonged to the Shaw family, who kept a watchful eye over their youthful charges. "The coasting hill was patrolled carefully by my father-in-law. He built two ski jumps from which all the young people would learn. Trees were cleared to make the hill safe for coasting. In 1961 my husband gave the coasting hill to the Conservation Land Trust. Before automobiles, they used to bobsled to the road from the top of the hill. Even after automobiles came, the town after a good snowstorm would not allow cars, so children could use the hill as a coasting area. My mother-in-law was a Hutchins and her family came from Punkatasset Hill on Monument Street. My husband's uncle, Gordon Hutchins, was very firm that his coasting hill be used only for skiing and toboggans and sleds were forbidden. The two relatives would kid each other when they would meet on the propriety of allowing coasters."

Leif Nashe arrived from Trondheim, Norway, over seventy years ago at the age of twelve with his mother and older sister to join his father here. He was already familiar with ski jumping. Norwegians, he says, began arriving in Concord in 1873, many from Loiten, and brought their knowledge of skiing and ski making with them. He attributes the first pair of skis made in Concord to Lars Petersen in 1876. Peter Seversen, he says, during the 1880s and 1890s, began making skis for the

Helen and Walter K. Shaw, Jr. 1967. (Courtesy of Gordon Shaw)

sporting goods stores in Boston, and Anton Hoff continued this in the early 1900s. Nashe himself, with partner Odd Overgaard, built upon this tradition with the successful establishment of Dovre Ski Binding on Beharrell Street.

Even the formidable Judge Prescott Keyes of the Concord District Courthouse could have a bit of fun giving the boys in the area rides through ropes attached to his Stanley Steamer. Jim Powers remembers being one of those kids grabbing onto the long ropes of the Judge's car after a big sleet storm and being taken all over town. "It was amazing to me that the very famous judge would do a thing like that. He was as human as could be."

And after a winter's snowfall, with few sidewalks then, David Little recalls the town pungs carrying their sand and gravel. He describes the pungs as boxlike wagons on double runners with the front runners used to steer the horses, and connected to an axle and pole that pivoted. Little had a better chance of hopping a pung if he was with his mother. "My mother had gone to school with a number of the drivers, and they would stop and wave and ask her if she wanted a ride. She would sit with the driver in the box and I would be hanging on the rear runner."

Anne Newbury was one who took her chances on the pung of Theophilus Mason, the iceman. "He had a big pung with wide runners, so it was easy to get on and off and we'd run along with him off and on. He was very kind to us till we'd get way, way from home. Then he'd whip up his horses and go like mad, sometimes throwing us off and leaving us a long ways from home." Living along Lowell Road, Newbury and her friends enjoyed the skating on the nearby ice pond. "An ice house was located there and we would skate around the holes that were made as they were cutting the ice."

For the young Boy Scout, Peanut Macone, winter was the time to skate to Fairhaven Bay with his troop. "Very cautiously we crossed under the bridges by way of a rope, because the water is quick under the bridge. Our scoutmaster, Bebe Hosmer, had a program in which we took ladders, lifesavers, and ropes to several easy spots, where skaters or others in need could get to them. We spent the afternoon playing hockey and came home exhausted but with happy memories."

All Summer Long: Space to Explore, Reflect

In a world more akin to Huck Finn than to that of today's youth, the openness of Concord's woods, rivers, and meadowland beckoned endlessly for exploration.

"It was a wonderful childhood," recalls Dr. William Davis. "We used to make our own fun and spent a lot of time in the woods or along the river from Fairhaven Bay to the Carlisle bridge. We were independent and free, enjoying canoeing and camping. William Brewster, who owned the October Farm on Monument Street, was a naturalist who had campsites along the river. We used the river a lot and I did a great deal of studying there."

"Times used to be," says Bill Towler, "that when I went up the street, I knew everyone. I could go to any house and knock on doors and walk in. I'd sit down for a glass of milk and a story and I'd tell them what was going on downtown." Towler and his friends would go down to the Millbrook

56   When We Were a Couple of Kids

and find whiskey bottles and sell them to the drugstores. "We'd get two or three cents per bottle, then go over to Towle and Kent's grocery and buy two or three cents worth of broken cookies which we'd sit down beside the curb and eat."

Elmer Joslin and his friends were eager participants in this recycling effort, knowing that many a bottle had been placed in the horse stalls outside the First Parish Church. Swapping them for candy with the local druggist meant one penny's worth for a half pint up to a nickel for the rare quart bottle.

There were the soda fountains at Snow's and Richardson's pharmacies, where Towler could get "fizz"—ground ice with strawberry and raspberry syrup. Whitney Smith called his shaved ice in a glass with flavored syrup poured over it a "freeo." With an abundance of fruit grown in the area, Towler admits that he and his friends were not the least bashful about taking their share. "You'd be walking up Nashawtuc Hill and any kid could lean right over and grab the apples."

"As kids we made our own pleasures," says Joslin. "We learned to swim in the Concord River where we put a little indentation in the bank. The test was that if you were able to swim across and get through

the water lilies and back to that point, you were lucky. We later went down to Main Street to the South Bridge, where the boat house is, and swam there. If you were a good swimmer, you could dive from the trestle into the river, but I never did like the high diving business."

"When the river was too low and warm to be refreshing, we went to Walden," says Laurence Richardson. "Sandy Beach, near the pond, required bathing suits, but Thoreau's Cove and Sam Hoar's point nearby was free country and all you needed was a bicycle to spend a happy day there."

"In those days we swam in the clothes God gave us," adds Joslin, "but the gypsy moths one year had eaten the leaves off the trees between the road and pond at Walden, so we had to give that up and moved over to Thoreau's Cove and built a dock and swam there. But as more automobiles came into town and people wanted to see the site of Thoreau's hut, they would be in the woods near where we would swim. I was caught in the pond many times with my clothes on shore."

Lake Walden was a stop on the railroad and groups of people regularly came up from Boston for a day's outing. Joslin remembers some rowdiness among the groups that arrived, some bathtub liquor brought along and occasional drownings. "It was customary then for the Concord Independent Battery to fire several charges at the water's edge to bring the body to the surface. I remember seeing this done several times." Joslin adds that bathhouses

A pung from the J.D. Murray grocery store speeds down Academy Lane. Circa 1900. (Courtesy of the Concord Free Public Library)

58 When We Were a Couple of Kids

stood over the water; a dance hall, located at the opposite end of the railroad siding, was later destroyed by forest fire; and there were refreshment stands and a bicycle track.

Elsie Kennedy and her companions would ride double on bicycles to get to Walden and she laughs when she looks at the photos of the bathing suits of her girlhood days. "Can you imagine getting all this clothing wet?" she asks, pointing to the sleeveless swim dress over bloomers with rolled stockings, which she dates around 1920. The one piece woolen bathing suits for both men and women came into style later in the decade and Kennedy remembers the furor over men going topless. Swimwear designers accommodated the transition by placing a zipper along the waist of the trunks to allow men to add

At Walden Pond. Elsie Kennedy, second from left, with friends. Circa 1920. (Collection of the Concord Historical Commission, courtesy of Elsie Kennedy)

Officer Bob Lawson was called to quell the disturbance and instead joined the group that was determined to celebrate the town's birthday by rousing residents at dawn in 1930. One Boston newspaper covering the event described the group as a "squad of racketeers making the rounds at daybreak, leaving no street untraveled." Left to right: Front row kneeling—John Robinson (with stick), Lloyd Howe, unidentified employee of Charlie Mason, John Martinson, Harold Hansen, Charlie Voigt, Jesse Potter, Bob MacLeod, George Nelson, Peanut Macone, Bill Tibbetts, Tommy Tombeno. Standing—Bob Lawson, John Tombeno, Bing Bartolomeo, Jim Powers, Charlie Mason, Bill Wilson, Walter Hansen. (Courtesy of Robert MacLeod)

En route to Walden Pond on a barge for a birthday party. Mary Chamberlin wears a white bow, and next to her is Gladys Clark in the white hat. 1908. (Collection of the Concord Historical Commission, courtesy of Gladys Clark)

or remove the top, she explains. Kennedy was the first instructor through the Red Cross to teach swimming to children at Walden in 1927. "Two years earlier, with the encouragement of Mary Pratt, a Red Cross member and a registered nurse, the program was begun at White Pond. Within two years it outgrew the facilities and was transferred to Walden Pond."

As one of eight children, Anne Chamberlin Newbury had a lively time growing up here. "We seemed to know almost everyone. In the summer we would go to Lake Walden to swim. We would start at the top of the hill of what we called 'the point' and run down and dive into the pond because the shore went off quite steeply right there. We also swam at White Pond. We tramped all over the town, we knew it from one end to the other. We knew the rivers and took picnics and went off for the whole day. There was no organized activity for the young at that time so we would have pickup games of baseball anywhere in town."

There were always plenty of Smiths to play with, she adds, and Farnham Smith, who lived at Academy Lane, agrees. He grew up in an extended family of grandparents, aunts, uncles, and cousins who lived close by on Middle Street, Main Street, and Sudbury Road. "We were in and out of each other's houses constantly and together in all manner of family gatherings." Living so close to the depot, a special interest of Smith and his neighborhood friends were the railroad trains and the names on the Pullman and freight cars. This interest in the railroads, he adds, has stayed with him all his life.

Smith was in high school when the 1918 influenza epidemic struck and with so much sickness, he recalls, the staff at the depot was down to Mr. George Hunt, the stationmaster. "He knew me because of my interest and my hanging around the station and asked if I would like to try handling baggage while he was so shorthanded. As a result for almost four weeks, with the high school closed, I was the baggage master, receiving pay from the federal government, then running the railroads during the war, in sums of money that sounded pretty big to me in those days."

To Polly Kussin, growing up in Concord meant "experiencing freedom from confusion, noise, and cars. Bicycles were the common means of transportation and we used to ride them very fast up and down Main Street." Kussin grew up in the Thoreau-Alcott house at 255 Main Street, where her grandmother Anna Bronson Alcott, who was Meg of *Little Women,* lived. "We had a good yard in the back of our house for playing such games like 'ally, ally over,' and baseball and track meets were eagerly watched. Our friends were a close-knit group of girls and boys, some of whom I would continue to know throughout my life."

Elizabeth Babcock had plenty of space to roam in the fields of the Simon Willard farm where she grew up on Nashawtuc

Elizabeth Babcock. 1978. (Photo by Alice Moulton)

Hill. "A stone on Elm Street told us about the early settler Simon Willard and I couldn't help but be aware early on as a child that Concord was a place where great things had happened in the past. Before I could read the stone, my father told my sister and me what it said and we sat there on the two boulders or slabs of granite, which were sort of shoulders for that stone, and we snuggled up to Simon Willard."

Babcock remembers waking up to the sounds of cattle coming up Elm Street that were being taken to New Hampshire for the summer and the wagons taking their produce into the Boston market. "The surrounding meadows became a great place for acting out the Knights of King Arthur, even waylaying some people who were wandering by and challenging them to battle, most of them proper matrons walking up Elm Street." Intruding on this, says Babcock, was a certain awareness that there might be danger for a young girl to be in the woods alone. "I was very aware that the reformatory did exist and I was probably conditioned a bit by the fact that my father was the United States marshal for this district. I was too young to have remembered much of it but we did have to have the house on Nashawtuc Hill guarded. A little railway went from the reformatory to Boston via the woods which was a possible escape route for inmates."

Charlie Byron remembers doing a lot of roaming around Lake Walden where the old railroad station used to be and where the picnic grounds were located across the tracks. "In the late fall we would set our traps, but I could never bring myself to skin an animal, so I had to pay somebody else to do it. We would hang the hides on the chicken house that we had in the backyard." Mark Mara did a lot of trapping with his friend Robert Parke. "We had between 250 and 300 traps on the Concord, Sudbury, and Assabet rivers and also trapped on land. We used to take about forty muskrats a day from the rivers and from the Millbrook, which was loaded with muskrat, mink, and fish."

Jim Powers and his friends used to pick up spare money by trapping. "Muskrats, skunks, mink, and raccoons were plentiful, and trapping was quite a big business among the young fellows. That's where we got our pocket money. In those days, we'd get $2.50 for a muskrat skin, the same for a skunk, and $18.00 for a mink, so we spent a lot of time in the river trapping and fishing. I seemed to have grown up in a canoe, but I never swam in my life. Isn't that strange? I tipped over a number of times and I just grabbed the canoe.

"The hurdy-gurdy man would come around and crank his music out, sometimes having a little monkey with him. The rag man was a favorite of the children and he had a horse and wagon that went around as he picked up rags and bottles. We kids would try to find bottles because he would be around on Saturday and we would try to sell them to him for two cents a bottle, which meant more pocket money for us."

Mark Mara, like many other boys, worked on the surrounding farms. He describes the routine when he worked on his uncle's farm, the Colonel Barrett farm on Barrett's Mill Road. "We used to get there at 4:15 in the morning and take care of five teams of horses, clean the barn, wash the cows and start the milking at 5:00. We milked until 7:30 when we went into the house and ate breakfast with the other men who worked there by the month. At 8:00 you went out to work for the day, being back at the barn at 4:30 in the afternoon to wash and milk the cows again until 7:30, and then my uncle sent us home. For all that work, seven days a

Mark Mara. 1978. (Photo by Alice Moulton)

week, we got the great sum of twelve dollars, a chance to learn the business, and all the water you could drink."

But Mara was enterprising in capitalizing on the brisk tourist trade drawn to Concord's rich past and from the age of nine he was a guide at Sleepy Hollow. "We lived just across from the cemetery on Bedford Street and I learned all the graves of any note. I used to earn about forty or fifty cents a day by being alert and having a spiel, which the people were more amused with than what they learned." Joslin, too, tried his hand in the guide business. "In the summer there was money to be earned selling guidebooks, postcards, and showing people around the town. We would stand as close to the streetcars as we could to sell cards and books. Then a line was painted so many feet from the cars and we were not supposed to go beyond that line, but we would put our toe to the mark and reach over. I think that was probably the first traffic line painted on the streets in Concord."

The streetcars themselves were the wings of boyhood. "When we got on that streetcar," says Joslin, "we felt like the big shots of the town. On a Sunday afternoon instead of chasing around in the woods here, we raised fifteen cents to get to Arlington Heights and for another dime we could ride the whole afternoon on what was then the Boston Elevated. We knew how to change cars and how to pick up transfers and we spent the whole afternoon going all over."

The Town Hall, says Mara, was a main center of activity when he was a boy. "I attended my first dances here; there were basketball games, Punch and Judy shows, movies, and a balcony and stage on which plays were held." It is the simplicity of those childhood games that linger for Peanut Macone. "The fun we had creating our own play without any direction from older people. 'Ally, ally, over' was a good game because there were a lot of sheds behind the houses. Someone would throw a tennis ball over the shed and shout ally, ally, over. Somebody on the other side would catch it and then chase the opposing group around the shed, throwing the ball at

each one. When it hit someone, that meant they were captured. Hide-and-seek was another game we played quite a bit, and a lot of scrub baseball where we chose up sides that included both boys and girls. But for me it was the Boy Scouts that I enjoyed most about growing up and scoutmasters like Bebe Hosmer taking us into the woods for the day."

"We always seemed to know what to do," says Anna Manion. "We organized our own lives—there was no Little League or things like that. We played marbles, jump rope, hopscotch, and jackstone and enjoyed the neighborhood baseball games in the open fields together. When it got dark, mother had a policeman's whistle to summon us and no alibis were accepted. Everybody could hear that whistle."

In the summer it was a big treat for Manion to ride the train to Boston and take the boat to Nantasket Beach, swim there, ride all the attractions in the amusement park, and come home by boat and train all in the same day. "Riding the train to Boston was something we did often with our mother, walking up to Jordan's from North Station and back, and eating at one of the Ginter restaurants that we children thought were very swanky. My father always took us to Boston to the Barnum and Bailey Circus and of course we went to the smaller version at the cattle show here in Concord, and I'll never forget my nightmares from the first time I saw the snake charmer."

It was a time when peddlers passed through town regularly selling their wares with everything imaginable, says Manion, and for a time the gypsies made their annual visit, which frightened many. "We were told they would try to steal us when we were children and some mothers actually hid their children under the bed when they were around. They really just wanted to make money telling fortunes and selling baskets."

Fairhaven woods was an extension of Manion's neighborhood and meant a great deal to her youth. "We spent lots of time there, sometimes just walking and stopping for a drink from the cold spring, or picking blueberries when they ripened, climbing Thompson's cliff, and walking to the cove at Walden Pond to swim. It was there that we cut our annual Christmas tree, and in winter coasted and tobogganed down to the river below, that was usually frozen along the edges."

Gladys Clark felt there was a noticeable difference in the lives of children who lived in town from those like herself who lived in the country. "Children who lived in town took dancing and music lessons and had more of a social life among themselves living closer together. Out here in the country we were isolated and generally came to town only once a week. We spent our time playing with the farm animals. We had a goat, cows, rabbits, chickens, and I talked my father into letting me have a couple of pigs. While the children in town liked to come out here, it was a real luxury for me to get invited to go into town to play with someone or have dinner at the Colonial Inn. But this was when I was older and had my bicycle to ride there."

Her brother Dana drew on his country surroundings for his high school theme book. He found that the best time to study animal life to be on "a warm, rainy morning between five and six-thirty, covered with a dark overcoat to keep off the rain and to blend with the dark, dripping tree trunks." He watches "the bold walk of the fox, the rabbit blending harmoniously with the wet leaves and bushes" and writes of trapping young foxes on the ledge of Farmer's Cliff, stalking a woodchuck in the pasture, and with his rifle felling his prey.

With his book and rifle he stole away on a Sunday to his favorite nook in the woods, amidst deer, "some of which are very tame," and numerous squirrels. An early summer's afternoon would likely find him hitching the horse to the mowing machine and following it to throw the hay when it became too heavy for the machine. There is a sensitive appreciation of "sunset in an old New England Hill pasture, lowering over a grey stonewall and an orchard overgrown with juniper and barberries." And in "the dusky stillness," the youth feels "as though my soul had been purged and all the sins of the day forgiven."

For Anna Macone, who lived on nearby Lang Street, a walk through town brings back the memory of stopping off at Urquhart's bake shop for a chocolate éclair or going to the drugstore for an ice cream cone when each cost a nickel. It also brings to mind the sight of her beloved grandfather, Alessandro Macone, "a delightful little man with a big handlebar moustache who came from Italy and had twelve children. And when he took his produce from his farm on Strawberry Hill to market in Boston in a horse and wagon and returned the next morning, he would wait in town as we walked to school, with bags of peanuts ready for us kids."

5
Along the Rivers

To David Little, one of the greatest charms of Concord will always be its rivers. "It is the only place in Concord where your view is perhaps what it was 200 or 300 years ago. Canoeing in the early morning meant a great deal to me and helped me to face whatever the day might bring.

"I have been amphibious in and on Concord's three rivers since I was a small boy, long before I learned to swim. My first experiences were in a canoe with my father, who couldn't swim either. He taught me how to keep a canoe right side up; he was a strong and skillful paddler, and I loved to be in a canoe with him. Much of my early time on the rivers was less formal. A group of boys built rafts of railroad ties with a platform of lighter scrap lumber nailed on top. These rafts floated so low in the water that they were easy to climb back onto when we fell off, which was often. They moved slowly even when six boys were paddling them. We launched them into the spring floods when there was plenty of water over the meadows and also an occasional ice floe. We were soaking wet most of the time, even when we didn't fall off, but I don't remember that any of us ever caught cold from the exposure.

"My father didn't think much of these rafting voyages so, at mother's suggestion, he went to talk about them with Bebe Hosmer, a man who knew the rivers very well. 'Hell, Harry!' Bebe said, 'That boy can't drown! He's half Barrett, remember, and the Barretts have been marrying muskrats for two hundred and some years. Whoever heard of drowning a muskrat?'

"As I grew older I moved up to canoes rented from the South Bridge Boat House. We took day-long trips up and down the Sudbury and Concord rivers. The Damondale dam on the Assabet prevented us from going beyond it on that river. There were many picnic spots available then before the building boom of the last thirty years put houses on most of them. I remember particularly Martha's Point on what is now Conantum and the site of naturalist William Brewster's cabin at the foot of Balls Hill on the Concord River.

"My best years on the rivers began with the purchase of a two-seater kayak in 1950 which I kept in the South Bridge Boat House. One warm and sunny Washington's Birthday I went out with Bill Clark, rector of Trinity Episcopal Church. The boat house was closed for the winter but I knew of a weakly fastened window. If I were arrested for breaking and entering no one would be surprised, but Bill Clark clearly could not risk it. So I went through the window and passed my boat out to Bill. We paddled up the Sudbury River along a broad ribbon of open water between the ice-covered shores, noticing a colony of

68   Along the Rivers

dome-shaped muskrat houses on the flooded marsh. We paddled over to one of them. Bill thumped it with his paddle and gave his parish caller speech. No muskrat, alas, responded. We continued on upstream to the ice-closed entrance of Fairhaven Bay and watched people skating there.

"I told the Reverend Mr. Daniels, minister to the First Parish, about Bill's parish call on the muskrats and he let on to be furious. 'Why,' he said, 'all the muskrats on the Sudbury River are Unitarians; the Assabet and Concord River muskrats are Catholics. Bill Clark has no right to try to steal away our parishioners!' By 1961 I had added another kayak to my fleet, a short, broad-beamed fiberglass single-seater with a white hull and a red deck. She swished her stern from side to side with each stroke of my paddle and she made taffeta petticoat noises as she moved through the water. She tossed her male paddlers over her side at every opportunity but she never upset my wife. We named her *Marilyn*. I was allowed to keep her in the basement of a river-front house across Main Street from my home.

"*Marilyn* and I would get underway at dawn nearly every morning for an hour or so. The serenity I gained enabled me to rise above all the challenges of the day; the trip in and out of Boston, the office

---

The hemlocks on the Assabet. Circa 1900. (Courtesy of the Concord Free Public Library)

David Little. 1984. (Photo by Alice Moulton)

mail, and the telephone not least among them. Dawn is a busy time on the river. Muskrats are swimming about, their mouths full of waterweeds, lady mallards and wood ducks are convoying their ducklings to their breakfasts, snapping turtles are waiting to grab any stragglers.

"On summer mornings there is frequently a heavy mist arched over the river from bank to bank, hiding the shores and the way, ahead and astern, but revealing the sky and its clouds above. Seeing only the sky and clouds mirrored beneath my boat, I can tune my mind into believing that *Marilyn* and I are indeed floating high in the sky above the clouds, a delightful if dizzying sensation which lasts only until a snapping turtle sticks its head out of the water to look at us. I have never been able to imagine a flying turtle.

"One morning in such a mist I had just paddled under the Sudbury Road bridge when I heard a startled snort. I looked toward the sound and saw a sturdy buck deer standing knee-deep in the little canal that enters the river there. I talked to him gently as I do to wild creatures and we stared at each other for nearly a minute. Then he turned and climbed the bank through the thick bushes slowly and deliberately without cracking a twig. There is evidently still room for people and dogs and deer within the bounds of Concord.

"I watched a pair of huge snapping turtles making love one morning on the Assabet between Gibraltar and Pirates' Island. It was a very strenuous affair with much splashing about in midstream. What I remember best about it came at the end. One of the turtles came to the surface alone, stretched out its long neck, and sighed aloud. I had never heard a turtle make a gentle sound before.

"One advantage of my frequent appearances on the river was my acceptance by its residents as a harmless visitor. A wood duck family near Fairhaven Bay was especially cordial. The lady and her dozen ducklings would gather around my boat and make soft and cheerful sounds while I talked to them. I never fed them or any others of my friends on the river. I could address my remarks to one duckling and he would know that I was talking to him.

He would puff out his chest and swagger while the others looked at him and wondered what I thought he had that they didn't. Lady wood ducks are especially beautiful, their bright colors veiled under demure brown and gray outer feathers.

"The shallow Assabet is especially vulnerable to snags, fallen trees which often block the channel, causing unwary paddlers to try those snagless parts of the river strewn with hidden rocks. My son, Peter, and I have sawed up several large snags and brought them home for firewood. We rented a big aluminum canoe from the South Bridge Boat House and filled it with wood until only a few inches of freeboard remained. Then I demonstrated to Peter the stability of a heavy laden canoe by standing on one gunwale without tipping it. The Indians designed and built canoes to carry cargo but we use them very seldom for that purpose.

"Kayaking in the winter is very different. As dawn and the departure of my Boston train occur at about the same time, my winter kayaking was limited to weekends and usually to the Assabet, whose velocity opened up a channel sooner after a hard freeze than either the Sudbury or the Concord. By the time open water appeared its level was almost always lower than the

---

Fourth of July along Fairhaven Bay—a big day on the river featuring a parade of canoes. Circa 1900. (Collection of the Concord Historical Commission, courtesy of Stephen Smith)

level at which the river had frozen. I would board *Marilyn* at the shore edge of the ice, therefore, and coast down a gentle slope into the water. Persuading *Marilyn* to slide up that slope again at the end of our voyage was quite an undertaking as I did not dare to get out of my boat until she was over grounded shore ice. I had the river to myself in winter. Only an occasional hawk swung down to look me over. The ripples of my passage and the current tapped the thin ice on the edge of the channel to produce the tinkling sounds made by wind chimes hanging from the corner of a house. I could sometimes see animal tracks along the shore, but that was all.

"On summer weekends spectators on the bridges over our rivers are vastly entertained by the antics of the hundred or so visitors from out of town who rent canoes at the South Bridge Boat House. They have no idea how to paddle a canoe or how to steer one, but they do not seem to mind and they do indeed enjoy themselves. They are described as bank-to-bankers. Concord residents, furred and feathered as well as human, stay off the rivers during these invasions, but nothing dismays the snapping turtles."

On the Fourth of July

The river was a recreational area, a social center, and a street, recalls Laurence Richardson, and on the Fourth of July traffic there was heavy.

"The Fourth of July was a big day on the river for the Concord Canoe Club and the parade of canoes from Main Street to the Monument Street bridge," says Elmer Joslin. There were picnics and parties, wooden tub races, swimming meets, and canoe jousting. The tub races and the canoe jousting created the most havoc. "Usually both parties fell into the river, much to the amusement of the spectators gathered to watch the aquatic sports," remembers Harold Cabot.

"In the evening there was a carnival of boats with each boat or canoe lighted up with Japanese lanterns and the occupants dressed and posed to represent some idea or object such as Liberty or the Minuteman," describes Richardson. "The procession started from above the railroad bridge on the Sudbury River and ended below Monument Street on the Concord River. From where I was, the floats extended from Nashawtuc Bridge up around the bend of the river to Elm Street. Besides the canoes, the causeway and the North Bridge served as a grandstand for those who could not get to the big club piazza."

A Beacon to River Craft and to Whimsy

Those who live along the rivers often keep a canoe, rowboat, or other small craft in the back yard where it can be quickly launched for an excursion on the waterways. In most small, inland waterways, there have been few if any markers or navigational aids. One Concord resident who lived on the river did something about this and during its short life, the Nashawtuc lighthouse became a local attraction and a national curiosity.

Marian Miller relates that her husband Hans loved the theater and enjoyed doing things with a flair. And the Nashawtuc Lighthouse, while designed to serve a practical purpose, developed into good theater along the way. The Main Street home of the Millers bordered on the Sudbury River and when the water level became low during a dry spell, boats would be scraped by the rocks at the bottom. Any warning signs that they placed in the water soon drifted away and a red flag that they once placed from an overhanging branch also didn't last.

The summer of 1930 proved to be especially dry and created a very low water level in the river. Hans Miller was seeking relaxation in his garden by the river, puffing on his pipe when his serenity was shattered by the screech of an outboard motor, which had bent its propeller on the unseen ledge. It was then that he decided it was time to erect a permanent structure on the rock to prevent his garden from being "cluttered with rotting hulks of shipwrecked craft."

"What could be more interesting and beautiful than a lighthouse? My husband decided it should be straight, white, and colonial of course," recalls Marian. Holes were drilled in the offending rock into which upright iron rods were inserted and around which a large circular drum was placed to pour concrete. "It took most of the summer to build the frame of the lighthouse and plan for the wiring. The electric wiring ran from the lighthouse underground up to our house and into the cellar where it was attached to a switch run by our house current."

The Miller's fourteen-year-old son assisted his father, and Marian remembers him patiently listening to her husband's "grunts, heaves, and expletives." The materials for the lighthouse came from a variety of sources, but they were especially grateful for the interest and assistance offered through a friend who worked with the Edison Company in Lynn. "He made arrangements so my husband was given the necessary switches and equipment to produce a light which would go on exactly one minute after civil twilight and go off in the morning. In exchange, the Edison Company used a photograph of the lighthouse in its advertising."

The Millers set up a bulletin board to record the water level, wind velocity, temperature, time, and current. William Lincoln Smith, a professor of electrical engineering at Northeastern University, was asked to examine the wiring and structure. "He gave us a flowery testimonial to the effect that all was sound and has passed inspection," Marian laughingly remembers. "Invitations were sent to neighbors to attend the grand christening of Nashawtuc Light. Being a born actor, my

74 Along the Rivers

husband devised a costume which he considered appropriate to a commissioner, as he dubbed himself. Our neighbor, Bessie Millett, broke a bottle and we had a grand party."

The completed lighthouse stood fifteen feet high and people began to look for its welcome flash. Interest spread beyond Concord's boundaries. A writer for the *Boston Traveler,* Horton Edmands of Concord, included the following directions to his readers for viewing the lighthouse. "Go to the corner of Main and Nashawtuc Hill Road and take the road on which the town fathers have placed the sign, 'This road leads to no town.' Proceed towards 'no town' a few hundred feet and behold."

As far away as Freeport, Louisiana, they were reading of Concord's unique beacon of light. Hans Miller even had a letterhead made which said Nashawtuc Light, Boul-

der 88, Concord, and sent greetings to other lighthouses across the nation. Hans Miller's lighthouse was on its way to becoming a Concord landmark when the wet and cold winter season of 1936 arrived. Cakes of ice formed in the river and the water rose progressively higher.

Marian remembers that "the current was strong and ice cakes bobbed around menacingly. We went out with poles trying to push them aside." But the water became so high that it could no longer flow under the Nashawtuc Bridge. With the increased pressure, the cakes of ice pressing at the top of the lighthouse finally pushed it over. The lighthouse was tipped down into the muddy bottom of the river, taking the boulder with it. We never tried to right it and it still lies there, the rock upturned, still scraping canoes."

The Nashawtuc lighthouse, lighthouse keeper Hans Miller. Before 1936. (Courtesy of the Concord Free Public Library)

6
Ice Cutting

Ice cutting was an integral part of life and a familiar sight along such Concord ponds as Angier's, Bateman's, Fairhaven Bay, Warner's and Hayward Mill. The arrival of the iceman at local homes was the cause of great excitement for children who would gather around him eager to salvage any chips of ice that would fall from the truck after the ice was shaved to the appropriate size.

The family of John Forbes, who lived on Barrett's Mill Road, bought the ice business from Theophilus Mason, whose ice truck was a well known sight through town. Forbes relates that "the ice removed from the pond might often be eleven inches thick, twenty-two inches wide, and forty-four inches long. The average home would take about 100 pounds of ice which could be purchased for forty cents or fifty pounds for twenty-five cents."

Mary Ogden Abbott remembers "it was quite an outing to cut ice on Fairhaven Bay. It was always cut in front of my grandfather's boathouse and transported by sled to our ice house on Sudbury Road. When the ice melted or we ran out, I remember the iceman in his yellow cart bringing in the ice with his tongs on a rubber sheet over his back." And like many others, no matter how hard she tried to keep an eye on it, "the catch basin and trays for melting ice under the refrigerator were always overrunning."

Florence Damon recalls her husband's brother cutting ice at Hayward Mill Pond. "I can remember their coming with big saws and cutting the ice into great blocks which were floated down to the ice house. Sawdust was put between each layer to keep them from melting. He had his ice peddled by horse and team and people would put their card in the window to show they wanted ice. If they put the card one way, they wanted a ten-cent piece, another way, would be for a twenty-five cent piece." For the city boys who already had refrigeration and for those students from the south, watching Mike Ryan cut the ice at Bateman's Pond at the Middlesex School was an intriguing experience, relates Roger Fenn, who taught there. Indeed, the day when Ryan's team of horses fell through the ice and had to be rescued became a recurring topic of conversation.

And despite the inevitable replacement by refrigeration, the words of icemen like Forbes rings true, "a block of ice never gets out of order."

Ice cutting on Angiers Pond, off Strawberry Hill Road. Circa 1920. (Collection of the Concord Historical Commission, courtesy of Peanut Macone)

77   Ice Cutting

Herman Hansen with Theophilus Mason's ice
wagon in 1905. Mason's ice business was later
purchased by John Forbes of Barrett's Mill
Road. (Courtesy of the Concord Free Public
Library)

Elsie Kennedy's father Alfred and her uncle
Bert Loring with their ice wagon. Circa 1900.
(Collection of the Concord Historical Commis-
sion, courtesy of Elsie Kennedy)

7

School Barges and Scholars

As students they came to school on barges, were taught mainly by women who were required by the profession then to be maiden ladies, and attended a newly centralized public school system within Concord that replaced the district schools of their fathers.

Grammar school classes for students from Concord Center were divided between the Ripley School, where the Hunt Gym is now, the Peter Bulkeley building and the Emerson School, now the annex building. At Concord Junction, the West Concord School stood in the playground of the present Harvey Wheeler Community Center.

When the Harvey Wheeler School was built in 1918, it was the first in Concord to have all of its classrooms on a single floor. Each classroom had an outside door to permit quick evacuation of its pupils in case of an emergency. Florence Damon, who was then teaching at the nearby West Concord School, remembers many visitors from other school systems coming to look at it. Built of an attractive yellow brick, it was and is a very useful building.

The Harvey Wheelers offered to build a clock tower as an addition to the building,

says Damon, and that is how the school got its name. She was told that the bell in the clock tower was the bell from the Damon Mill that had called the workers to their jobs. When the Armistice news came that World War I had ended, she relates that there was great excitement. "The girl who was the physical education teacher and I climbed the tower and rang the bell. We were scolded afterwards, but it was great fun."

Damon's own career as a teacher ended when she married her husband Winslow in 1922. "No married teachers were permitted then," but as a member of the school committee from 1942 through 1951, she was actively involved in planning the construction of the Alcott and Thoreau schools. This was the first new construction of schools, since the high school had been built on Stow Street in 1929, and was the beginning of an era of growth which ended with the decade of the seventies and a declining school population.

The high school was located on Stow Street, where the parking lot for the Concord Free Public Library is now, and some residents remember the small building between the Emerson School and the high school, which was the Manual Training School. Students attending the high school came from Acton, Bedford, Boxboro, Carlisle, Lincoln, Littleton, and Sudbury. In the elementary grades they either walked to school, rode bicycles, or if they lived more than a mile away, rode on the horse-drawn barges. "In the winter the barge

Schoolboys ride past the West Concord School, taken down in 1944. Our Lady Help of Christians Church is alongside. Circa 1910. (Collection of the Concord Historical Commission)

The West Concord and Harvey Wheeler
schools. Circa 1920. (Courtesy of the Concord
Free Public Library)

Almira Pickard's seventh-grade class at the West Concord School. 1908. Left to right: Front row—Merton Hosmer, Harold Hall, Pliny Nims, Joseph Tallon, Albert O'Clare, Wilfred Thibeault, Sam Ross, Wilfred O'Clare. Second row—Leona Dye, Mary Castillin, Natalie Chapman, Margaret Prendergast, Margaret McEachern, Gertrude Williams, Ellen Reilly, Margaret Collins, Doris Jewett. Third row standing—John O'Grady, Almira Pickard—teacher, Neal McWilliams, John Brooks, Dorothy Pickard, Nellie Harmon, Ruth Damon, Harold Harvest, Edward McLeod, Sam Heyman, Dan Hays. (Collection of the Concord Historical Commission, courtesy of William Damon)

Florence Damon. 1978. (Photo by Alice Moulton)

was put on runners with hay placed on the bottom," describes Gladys Clark. "We used to freeze to death, those horses were so slow. The winters were agony. In the spring the curtains could be rolled up and on the last day of school, we would pick wildflowers and decorate the barges."

Years later when Clark became a teacher herself, getting to school was still no easy task during the winter. "I drove to school in an old Essex with no heat in the car and no automatic windshield wipers. I would start off in the morning with a hot water bag for my hands, heated bricks at my feet, and chicken wire, so if I went off the road, the chicken wire placed under the rear wheels would help get me back."

Students from West Concord came to the high school on the streetcar, Charlie Manion arrived with other students from Acton on the barge, and Gladys Clark remembers the students from Bedford and Lincoln arriving by train, with one boy from Carlisle driving down in his horse and carriage.

At the high school there were different courses of study which reflected areas of interest and aptitude, and to an extent class lines as well. "In the eighth grade," says Anna Manion, they decided what you were best suited for, and I was in the college course. There was a scientific course mostly for boys that was similiar to the college course, but with more science than we had. There was a general course, a domestic course for girls, an industrial arts course for boys, and a commercial course for those who wanted to go into office work."

Such division, however, limited student contact. "Students made their friends in the same courses and there was not too much crossing of lines, which was too bad," says Manion. Charlie Comeau, who graduated in 1923, recalls that "some students taking the college or scientific course didn't think the mechanical or domestic arts students were their equals." But his graduating class of 100 students, the largest at that time, has become a close-knit group, holding reunions every five years. Athletic expenses weren't an issue then, and Terry McHugh, who graduated in 1914, says "there were no gyms and al-

School barges in winter. Circa 1900. (Courtesy
of the Concord Free Public Library)

86 School Barges and Scholars

most no expense to athletics. Fifty-cent dues were paid to the athletic association with everyone providing their own uniforms."

In an era when corporal punishment was used in the schools, Mark Mara knew the sting of the rattan all too well. "The rattan was a long stick and two teachers would hold your arm out if you were balky. You would have to open your hand and they would belt you across the knuckles. It was better to take it on the palm of your hands. I got that almost every day. Miss Legate, the principal of the Peter Bulkeley School, years later told me that I was the worst behaved boy that she ever had in over fifty years."

Formidable, even terrifying, in student recollections, Miss Helen Legate taught the eighth grade and was the principal when Gladys Clark attended the Peter Bulkeley School. "We were scared to death of her. It was always a happy day when she was going into the office and the assistant had full swing. Though I survived the eighth grade, many who had gone through school with me did not. One after the other they had to stay back, stay back. The big boys left school at this point. When I saw them around town in later years, I thought they weren't so bad after all, they should have kept right on going. But oh, she was going to make perfection out of everybody."

Classroom at the old Ripley School on Stow Street. 1905. (Courtesy of the Concord Free Public Library)

Miss Legate lived in the Emerson House for many years with Miss Ellen Emerson and another teacher, Miss Grace Heard, whom Clark describes "as the inspiration of my life." Clark's bouts with whooping cough and rheumatic fever in the third grade had slowed her down considerably, and it was not until the fifth and sixth grades when Heard was her teacher that she was able to catch up. "She filled me with stories of the Greeks and Romans and good literature. Those years gave me a focus and encouraged me to do everything else better."

Two memorable lifelong career teachers, relates Clark, were the sisters, Abby and Jane Hosmer. "They lived on Lowell Road in the house just over the bridge on the right-hand side and were known throughout Concord as the Hosmer girls. They were marvelous teachers, tutoring right into their eighties. Anyone who was going to college or was failing went to the Hosmer girls to get brushed up in their education."

Anna Manion similarly remembers the Findeisen sisters, Minna and Maude. "They were excellent teachers. I had Minna in the sixth grade and Maude in the eighth. Everyone was a little afraid of Minna because she used to throw things. She would throw a book or pitchpipe at us, which made for a little excitement. She couldn't sing herself but expected us to do wondrous things."

"The high esteem and respect in which the teachers were held seemed to be the order of the day," observes Laurence Rich-

Concord High School classroom on Stow Street.
1905. (Courtesy of the Concord Free Public
Library)

Terry McHugh with his 1908 seventh-grade class taught by Emma Clahane, at the Emerson School. Left to right: First Row—Alice Potter, Josephine Moreau, Agatha Parmenter, Margaret Dee, Ella Anderson, William Tobin. Second Row—Arthur Anderson, Richard Swann, Gertrude Moody, Edward Clahane, Katherine Ryan, Sarah Towler, Terry McHugh. Third Row—Peter Feehan, Frank Coy, Murray Miner, Joseph Hanlon, William Kennedy. (Collection of the Concord Historical Commission, courtesy of Terry McHugh)

ardson. "Our teachers were of the best, those in the high school mainly graduates of Wellesley, Smith, Mt. Holyoke, and Radcliffe. And they stayed so long, they knew whole families, having taught them all from the oldest to the youngest and sometimes the parents as well."

"All of Concord was our gym," relates Anne Newbury, who graduated from Concord Academy as one of eleven students in the class of 1929. "We were out in the fields, skating across the meadows and all over town when we divided up to have our hare and hound chases."

Her mother, Anne Bixby Chamberlin, laid the groundwork for the Academy when she began a school for young children in her Lowell Road home using the Montessori method. The school expanded, says Newbury, to include more grades and was moved to Belknap Street and then to the building owned by the Daughters of the American Revolution on Lexington Road, where her mother named it Concord Academy. Chamberlin's efforts are all the more remarkable, when Newbury explains that her mother was totally deaf as an adult and learned to be an excellent lip reader, who taught the skill to others. "My mother had graduated from Wellesley College at a time when few women went to college. She felt strongly that girls were as brilliant as boys and should have greater educational opportunity available to them."

As the school expanded and the search for a new site became necessary, Chamberlin found the required committee work increasingly difficult with her deafness and ended her formal association with the Academy. The Samuel Hoar House on Main Street was chosen for the new location, and Concord Academy opened there in 1922. Newbury was in the sixth grade at the Academy, the year the new quarters opened, and has watched the school grow from a local to a national institution. There were boarders at the Academy from the very beginning, she recalls, and on Saturdays they were a familiar sight having their picnics on Punkatasset Hill. In her seven years at the Academy, Newbury remembers firm discipline, high standards, "we just didn't misbehave," and a great deal of emphasis on school spirit.

Barely twenty years old, Roger Fenn stepped off the train in Concord in 1915 en route with his bags to teach science at Middlesex School, founded in 1901 by headmaster, Frederick Winsor. For the next fourteen years he taught at the Lowell Road school that to him was a large family. "The pupil-teacher relationship was informal, friendly, and natural. Unlike the public schools at that time, most of the teaching staff were men and we all lived in the dorms together. There were about twenty-five boys with one married teacher and his family living at one end of the building and one unmarried teacher

---

Anne Chamberlin Newbury, fourth row, second left, with June 1928 Concord Academy student body. (Collection of the Concord Historical Commission, courtesy of Anne Chamberlin Newbury)

with his room in the same area as the students. We all took cold showers in the morning before breakfast and bedtime was usually at ten in the evening."

The boys, he says, liked to play pranks on the teachers, pranks of the ingenious rather than malicious variety. He remembers one instance when the school tower clock struck thirteen at midnight one evening. "I thought I had miscounted, but when I asked the other teachers the next day, they too heard the same thing. We all listened carefully the next night and when it struck thirteen, we decided to investigate and found that the bell had several spots or marks on one side of it, closest to the third story window of the boy's end of the dormitory. So this suggested looking in that boy's room while he was at class, and a rifle was found with a silencer on it that he had fired just at the last stroke of midnight."

Fenn remembers the pride he had initially taken in the behavior of the boys in his dormitory, who during the study period after dinner were always found dutifully in their rooms with their books. "The other teachers complained they couldn't keep their boys in their rooms. But one day I discovered a wire coming out the window of one of the boys' rooms. I traced it along the building to the boardwalk and found it

The first Middlesex faculty, 1901–1902. Left to right: John Chase, Shirley Kerns, founder Frederick Winsor, William Taylor, David Baldwin, Reginald Howe, Jr. (Courtesy of the Middlesex School)

connected to two pieces of metal, which, when walked across, touched and set off a buzzer in the hall. I now realized my boys were roughhousing instead of studying and when I walked across the boardwalk, the buzzer signalled them to dash to their rooms."

But not to be outdone, Fenn deadened the buzzer by placing a piece of cardboard inscribed "April Fool" between the two pieces of metal. "The next day I walked across the boardwalk into the building and right into a howling mob in the hall. They all ran into their studies and I said nothing, trying to scowl without smiling, and went on to my room. They got the point."

His future wife, Eleanor, was a close friend of Headmaster Winsor's daughter, and she would come out to the school to spend weekends there. It was not proper, she relates, to play tennis then in Concord on Sunday, but Winsor gave them special permission to do so as long as they chose a court away from the road, so as not to be seen.

With the belief that there should be a private school in town to offer younger boys the opportunities that Middlesex School did for older boys, Fenn pursued the goal of creating a school of his own. The public elementary schools had a predominantly female faculty, unable to coach young boys in athletics and group games which Fenn believed were so important to character building and learning sportsmanship. "The large classes of the public schools could not provide the close, friendly, easy relationship between teacher and student and be able to focus their teaching styles on the needs of individual students."

When a five and a half acre farm on Monument Street became available in 1928, Roger and Eleanor purchased the property. And while still teaching at Middlesex, Fenn set about the task of preparing the school to open for the 1929 academic school year. He hired a promising young architect, William F. Kussin, to design the school buildings. It was his wish to found a non-profit institution run by a board of trustees rather than a proprietary school. He succeeded in finding a board of trustees and enough parents who agreed with him "that the time was ripe for such an institution."

The design of the classrooms reflected Fenn's philosophy of education. "Each classroom was set up to accommodate ten to twelve boys, with chairs placed around the table for discussion purposes rather than having the teacher stand in front and propound his principles. We wanted a give and take between student and teacher and for the student to learn how to work out the answer. The student was not to be likened to a tank of gas in an automobile to be filled by the teacher, but instead had to come to school and develop the habits necessary to get his own education." He saw a strong comparison between the school boy and the colonial adult in 1775, "who left his plow and stood at the bridge facing the British troops for the opportunity to run his own government as a free citizen. Running his government was up to

him and his responsibility. And so in our school, getting an education was up to the boy, and we took the motto, *Sua Sponte,* which means 'on his own responsibility,' writing it under the picture of the statue of the Minuteman at the bridge for our emblem."

It was with fifty-three young boys and "high hopes" that the Fenn School opened on 25 September 1929. "Prosperity lasted just a few weeks before the stock market fell as it had never done before and the Great Depression was upon us. We were so involved in running the school that we didn't realize what a serious situation it was."

Tuition for day students then was $400 a year. The student body for many years was divided, with one-third day boys from Concord, one-third day boys commuting, and after the first few years, one-third as boarding students paying up to $1,250 a year. Fenn attributes his school's survival that first year to the ability of his staff to stay within their allocated budget and "the parents who were extremely loyal to us and paid their tuition bills on time."

When graduation day came in June of 1930, "several of the trustees came up close, nudged me, and whispered, 'how much do you need to get you through financially?' I had the pleasure of telling them, 'absolutely nothing.' "

Roger Fenn, in center, sits with faculty and students in June 1930 at the completion of the Fenn School's first academic year. (Courtesy of the Concord Free Public Library)

8

Ruts in the Road

It was a pioneering era, a time of transition from horse-drawn to motor vehicles, when Elmer Joslin began his career in 1916 with the Department of Roads and Bridges, which became the Department of Public Works. Located at the present site of Everett Gardens, the department was responsible for the town's roads and bridges and its engineering services. It was a career that would last forty years and it was during Joslin's tenure that the department converted from horses to trucks.

Almost all of Concord's roads when Joslin began were gravel, and flying stones and dust were a continuous obstacle for motor vehicles. Roads needed constant attention and were watered down with a cart that had two sprinklers at the rear of the wagon. "A man would put his foot on a lever and start the sprays going. This was a good way for boys to cool off in the summer as well."

The gravel itself varied in consistency from one town to another and Joslin explains that "attempting to lay a road surface was done on a hit or miss basis." Gradually gravel roads gave way to a macadam surface as heavy auto traffic created a need to spray with tar or asphalt. "To

hold the stones together, a hard wearable surface was needed. A workable tar was sprayed with a large truck to lay the dust and form an outer crust. In this way, a semi-permanent surface was laid." But laying a workable tar was no easy task. What would work in one part of town would not necessarily work in another because of the variation in the consistency of the gravel surface.

During Joslin's superintendency that began in 1920, at a salary of $2,400, he was a familiar figure touring the town in his Chevrolet coupe, and was often heard whistling as he checked the potholes and road ruts while bringing Concord into the automobile age.

There are Concordians who still recall the days when after a winter's snowfall there was no place to go, even if they could shovel a path out of their yards. "No attempt was made to plow the roads until 1917 when I bought a steel plow for the town," says Joslin. The steel plow was attached to the front end of a truck and that pushed the snow away to the side of the road.

This was not an easy task since tire traction was poor and chains had not been developed to increase the traction. "We even tried putting two trucks together in tandem fashion in the hopes of getting more traction, but this did not prove satisfactory." Eventually, the manufacturers developed chains suitable for use on the rear wheels of trucks. With snow plowing such

Elmer Joslin. 1978. (Photo by Alice Moulton)

this way, and only a six-to-eight-inch snowfall would make breaking the roads a worthwhile effort." One familiar team of horses that used to break out the roads be-

Road construction along Bedford Street. Circa 1918. (Collection of the Concord Historical Commission, courtesy of the Department of Public Works)

a laborious task, no attempt was made to plow all the streets in town. The only roads opened were the main arteries and according to Joslin, many people who owned automobiles prior to 1926–27 put their cars up on jacks in the fall and left them there until spring.

Before plowing, farmers "broke out" the roads in their vicinity. This was done, says Joslin, by putting a six-by-six foot timber just ahead of the rear runners of a two-runner sled with either two or four horses ahead of it. A path was opened and the snow leveled by spreading out what had fallen. "Actually, no snow was removed in

longed to the E. A. Comeau Company, whose first contract with the town began in 1904 and continued through the mechanized era of snow clearance until a few years ago when the company ended this aspect of the family business.

While the early snow plows had a straight blade, experimentation showed that a curved blade could push and slide the snow to the side of the road better. Over the years, tractors have been developed that can push efficiently through any depth of snow, a far cry from Joslin's struggles.

9

When the Motor Car Was All the Rage

By and large car models are pretty standard fare in this day of mass ownership. Save for an occasional customized detail, there's nothing special about watching the traffic go by, observe some longtime residents who remember when the sight of a car turned heads and seemed to reflect the individuality of their owners.

The strong-willed Judge Prescott Keyes embodied the new spirit according to those who remember him driving around in his Stanley Steamer. The Stanley twins, Freeland Oscar and Francis Edgar Stanley, had designed a steam car and opened their Newton factory in 1899. Reputedly the skilled mechanics they hired imparted their own individuality to the cars they made, so that no two Stanley Steamers were ever the same.

But then, many believed, no one was quite like the Judge, who in the course of his years presided over the Concord District Court, was president of the Middlesex Insurance Company, a leading figure with the Concord National Bank, Town Moderator for many years, and by all accounts

an influential individual about town. "The Judge said precisely what he meant," remembers David Little, "and sometimes a little more strongly than was needed. There were those that feared him and even those that hated him, but he was a man of his word, who didn't suffer fools gladly."

But he was a favorite of the Macone children, whose father Nick had a garage business on Lowell Road and took care of the Judge's cars. "He carried Hershey bars that he would give out to us kids, and I don't know why they didn't melt," says Anna Macone. Her brother, Peanut, remembers that, during the time the Judge was head of the Middlesex Insurance Company, it would take him six turns around Monument Square to build up enough steam to get the car really moving.

Chick Edgarton was one of the young boys who could count on the thrill of being towed on his iceskates when the meadows flooded and froze, holding on to the long rope the Judge threw out attached to the Stanley Steamer. With the Steamer using kerosene as fuel instead of gasoline, there were those who maintained they could smell a Steamer before they saw one. During World War I, with the need to conserve gasoline, Edgarton remembers the Judge riding around with the sign, "I burn kerosene not gasoline."

The Judge's wife, Alice, adds Peanut Macone, had an electric car, which, when parked at their home on the corner of Main Street and Nashawtuc Road, "gave out an eerie blue light that would shine

100   When the Motor Car Was All the Rage

Peanut Macone. 1978. (Photo by Alice Moulton)

through the windows, which was mystifying to many people but kept the car charged for when it was taken out on the road." Mary Wheeler was an ardent fan of the electric car, buying them into the 1930s. "Many times," laughs Peanut, "her car would run down some miles from home and we would have to tow her home, giving her all sorts of reasons why the battery ran down. I don't think the electric car could go more than thirty-five or forty miles on one charge."

Judge Prescott Keyes and his wife Alice wait in their Stanley Steamer for a parade to begin. 1905. (Collection of the Concord Historical Commission, courtesy of Peanut Macone)

Considered a superb craftsman in building canoes in the area, George Warren was one of the first owners of the early cars. "George Warren, believe me, was one of the town characters," says Peanut. "I love characters, I'm one myself. George willed a Model T Ford to my dad." Anna adds that it was a 1923 Model T that he had bought for about $400 from their father's garage. "My dad later gave the car to me and I still have it. It has a convertible top, like a one-horse shay, with side curtains on. In the car was a collapsible jack and lots of little gadgets. There is no door on the left side of the car because the spare tire is there so you have to crawl in from the side. It's called a runabout and seats two people and was the first year for the self-starting car.

Anna Macone. 1980. (Photo by Alice Moulton)

I have the duster and hat that people used to wear to keep the dust off of their clothing. My dad taught me to drive when I was thirteen and I got my license at sixteen—there weren't too many girls driving then."

Nick Macone's garage was the site of the Old Nick Club, where some of the earliest models were kept by their owners, from late April to December first. Peanut still has a copy of the formal constitution, designating the means of paying his father, that was drawn up in 1906 and signed by its members.

To Gladys Clark's father, the sight of the early horseless carriage was one of wonder mixed with apprehension at what his horse would do. "I remember the first automobile that appeared on Lowell Road. My father came dashing into the house, calling us all to come look at the horseless carriage. If one approached while we were riding in our carriage, he made everyone get out and over the stone wall while he held the horse's head down to calm it." And as more and more automobiles came into use, explains Clark, the demand increased for better roads, and many of the existing stone walls were taken down and crushed for the macadam roads being built.

They were pioneers then in their driving machines that would revolutionize travel, redefine mobility, eclipse distance, and unify formerly separate areas of town.

10

Clang, Clang, Clang Went the Trolley

The clanging of the streetcar reflected a tempo of life as well as a popular means of transportation during the first quarter of this century. Local residents who rode the cars within Concord often speak about them with a sentiment that is seldom associated with today's modern conveyances.

Service began on the Concord & Clinton Street Railway and on the Concord, Maynard, and Hudson Street Railway in 1901. The following year the two lines consolidated. The last streetcar ran in Concord in 1923, by then the appeal of the private automobile had become strong.

In a less hurried day there was time for conversation with the conductor of the trolley, says Joseph Dee. The streetcar tracks ran in front of his home on Bedford Street and their schedule could be depended on. "If you wanted something downtown—a loaf of bread or a newspaper—you could ask the motorman to get it for you on the way back. There would often be time for a little chitchat with you, while the passengers sat there as calm as they could be. That's the way life was then."

For the young child there was a special excitement when the streetcar passed the house, particularly during the quiet of the evening hours. It is a feeling that has stayed with Adeline Cabot throughout the years. "When I was ten years old, I lived in the house on Main Street, where the headmaster of Concord Academy lives now. I used to go to bed and listen to the night sounds, which were very few then. Way down on the Milldam I would hear the rattling and clanging of the streetcar and when it actually went by my house to go down Sudbury Road, well that would be the big moment of the evening."

In town, where Boyd's real estate firm is now, was the waiting room for the streetcars. Through a system of transfers, a nickel would take a passenger a long way. It was possible for twenty cents to go from Concord to Hudson, with transfers that passed through four fare zones. At Monument Square connections were made with the Bedford-Concord branch of the Lexington & Boston Street Railway for Bedford, Lexington, and Arlington Heights. At Bedford connections could be made for Billerica and Lowell; at Lexington for Waltham and Woburn; and at Arlington Heights with the Boston Elevated Railway cars for Cambridge, Somerville, and Boston. Connections at Hudson could be made for Marlboro, Clinton, Worcester, and Fitchburg.

It was this relative ease of travel that enabled people to go farther than they had

A choice of trolley lines and destinations
brought a new found freedom to travel for
many. The open trolley was used in the summer months. Circa 1910. (Courtesy of the Concord Free Public Library)

before. A popular day's outing was to Lexington Park, which is remembered as an excellent amusement park. And by permitting people to go beyond the confines of the town on their own, the electric streetcar gave women a sense of greater independence, adds Gladys Clark. Mark Mara sold newspapers to the passengers aboard. "The motormen would see that I got home safely, in fact they would stop right across the street from my house. I used to sell my papers with a prepared spiel that went '*Boston Herald!* Three men killed but nobody hurt.' I got fifty cents a week for that."

In our day of rising gasoline prices, a search for parking, meters running overtime, and increasingly unpredictable train service, a look backwards can seem like an innovative glance.

11
When Hobos Passed Through

It was a common sight to see the drifter, the hobo, riding the freight cars and finding an odd job and meal wherever he could. A solitary figure, he found brief companionship with others like himself moving from town to town and has become somewhat romanticized in the folklore of our country. The disheveled, worn attire was compensated in the eyes of some by the chance to exercise complete freedom of mobility in the old spirit of the rugged individualist.

To Joseph Dee the biggest change in the life of the town was the loss of neighborliness. He began to see people living alongside one another and remaining strangers, their property protected by locks and elaborate security systems. Such times and such precautions could not welcome a hobo's presence. But when Dee was growing up along Bedford Street there was always wood to be chopped for the wood burning stove, and the hobos who stopped at his house proved to be willing workers for a meal. "It was usual for these hobo fellows to come along. They'd see the pile of wood in the back and come to the door and say they were hungry and ask if we wanted

some wood sawed or split. And we found they'd give good value too by working a couple of hours. My mother would call them in and give them a good meal and they would relish it. They told you they didn't know where or when their next meal would be, so they were grateful. And if they came back the next year, they knew where the soft spots would be."

Elsie Kennedy on Barrett's Mill Road lived close to the reformatory railroad station. "Because they used to follow the railroad, we saw a lot of them. My grandmother welcomed them, and she used to feed them in exchange for some work that they did. She always believed that they left some identifying mark around the barn to let those coming after them know they were welcomed here."

The sight of the hobos coming off the freight trains was a familiar one to Charlie Comeau. "My family was convinced that they marked the post in front of the house as a sign that they could get a meal there," he says. "My mother fed them outside the house in the backyard because she was afraid they would bring vermin inside. There was no fear of robbery or violence though, and I never heard of any incidents. Some slept under the bridges and built little fires. It was all a common sight for me."

Comeau distinguishes between the hobo drifter, whom his family found to be little interested in work and the seasonal transient workers who were often immigrants. "My father would give them a job either on the farm or in his construction business. There were many boarding houses in town for these laborers and those working in the factories here who needed a room. A number of laborers came from Nova Scotia in the spring. And when they arrived people around here would say, 'Guess the mud has dried up in Nova Scotia.' They were used to driving oxen and made good teamsters driving our horses."

Comeau also mentions another group that commonly passed through town—the traveling pack peddlers, some of whom were women. Carrying their wares, they doggedly went from place to place trying to sell shoe polish, laces, pins, or needles. They too have become a vanishing species. It was all part of the American landscape then, says Comeau—just another way of life.

12

The Boys of Baseball

Baseball once held an unrivaled place in the recreational life of the community. From backyard games to semi-pro events swelling crowds to the thousands at Emerson Playground, baseball was the dominant recreational pastime for Concordians.

"Outside of a movie now and then, baseball was the diversion in those days," recalls Brick MacWilliams. "It was a Saturday afternoon game and if it rained, the whole town went into mourning because everyone looked forward to those Saturday games."

For a time it was actually against the law to play ball on Sundays, says Terry McHugh of Lexington Road, born in 1897. "One Sunday I remember Billy Craig, the Chief of Police arriving and saying that he's got to take all our names because he received a complaint that we were playing ball. He took our names, and then told us to move some place out of sight of the road." Mark Mara was one of the boys who would watch out for the police. "We had lookouts posted and when a special police officer, like one grand man by the name of Emil Thorpe, was spotted, everyone would disperse."

McHugh, who went on to play semi-pro ball, continued playing well into his adult years. "The last team I played on was the Concord Town Team in 1926, part of the Middlesex Eight at that time." Baseball teams and leagues mushroomed throughout the town, representing neighborhoods and even churches. McHugh tells of playing with the "Asparagus League" which had the six teams of the East Quarter, the Depot, Herringville, Sleepy Hollow, Hubbardville, and the Holy Name Society of St. Bernard's. "We didn't have uniforms, just shoes and hats." Mara, from the Sleepy Hollow section, remembers the fun of "taking on the rough, tough boys from the Depot, whom we used to slow down sometimes."

And one of the few reasons a boy from West Concord would go "downtown," according to Archie Ferran, was to challenge the baseball team from Emerson Playground. Ferran's uncle, Archie Simpson, was manager of the Concord Junction team. MacWilliams remembers the teams of Concord Junction, the Westvale Athletic Association, the West Concord Juniors, and the Union Club which originated with the West Concord Union Church and formed about 1919. He also played semi-pro ball in the Middlesex Valley and the Paul Revere leagues. "Concord was a real baseball town and we used to draw some tremendous crowds. We looked forward to the battle between Concord Junction and Maynard, traditional rivals in almost everything. In Union Club days, since we

110   The Boys of Baseball

didn't have grandstands, the ladies used to bring their camp stools and parasols and line up on the base lines."

Charlie Comeau played semi-pro ball for ten years and remembers baseball being taken as serious business. "I recall the games with Maynard. Busloads of people arrived, a band was present, and there were even mounted police. If you struck out, you might not be spoken to for a week." It was the semi-pro games that brought the local Concord boys together with big league names, and according to Mara drew as many as 8,000 to 10,000 people to Emerson Playground on the weekend. Local team representatives would go into Fenway Park to see if the Red Sox or the visiting team had players who were not in the rotation and could be available for a weekend game.

There was the thrill, recalls Mara, of seeing the star pitcher of the New York Giants, Chick Davies, playing in Concord, or following the careers of Concord brothers, Al and Dick Loftus, who went on to play nationally. "Dick went on to pitch for the Brooklyn Dodgers and Al played in the Eastern League." Ferran adds that to find out the scores for the Boston big league games, they would go down to the railroad station and gather around the telegrapher for Western Union, who would tap out what was happening in each inning.

Alongside the big baseball events, many sandlot games took place throughout town. Jim Powers remembers playing baseball at the end of Belknap and Elsinore streets, in what had been the cattle show field where the circus used to come. "We just called what we played scrub. Scrub number one was the batter, scrub number two the pitcher, scrub number three the catcher, and so forth." And it was there at the fairgrounds that Ferran remembers the time when Billy Bulger batted the ball over the tent in back of the field and only got two bases.

They still speak of the ball games and the plays, men who are now in their seventies and eighties, but who will remain in memory the boys of baseball.

Members of the Knights of Columbus baseball team, turn of the century. Left to right: Martin Bulger, seated in center. First row—Mike McHugh, Mart Powers, John Goulding, Jim Hanley, Jerome Gleason. Second row—Jim Powers, Mike Powers, Bill Dee, Mark Mara. (Collection of the Concord Historical Commission, courtesy of Terry McHugh)

13

When Entertainment Was Close to Home

Curtain Going Up—The Early Days of the Concord Players

When Samuel Merwin turned his creative energies to starting the Concord Players in 1919, it became an organization that Marian and Hans Miller were readily attracted to when they moved to town the following year. For Hans it was the enjoyment of acting and for Marian it was an interest in makeup and backstage work.

Concord has always loved dramatics, she says, and the Concord Players acquired the assets and became heir to the two earlier efforts to establish local community theatre, both calling themselves the Concord Dramatic Club. The first, begun in 1875, lasted until 1900 and existed without formal organization or membership. The second club, begun in 1901, had officers, by-laws, and dues paying members and lasted until 1918.

At first the Players performed in private homes or in the Town Hall, she explains.

"The Town Hall, however, lacked a backstage and had a small performing stage. There was no place to store materials and costumes, and scenery continuously had to be carried around." The need was strong for a home of their own and Marian Miller was on the board when the present site of 51 Walden, then an old drill shed for the armory, was chosen. The architectural skills of her father, Clarence Blackall, were tapped and the stage he designed for the Players was a smaller replica of the one he did for the Colonial Theatre in Boston.

Monies were raised through subscriptions, says Miller, as well as through town appropriation; and after moving into their new home in 1922, the Players became increasingly ambitious about doing bigger plays and taking them to other places. "The most ambitious undertaking I remember was the performance of the play *Clarence,* with the famous tennis ace, Bill Tilden, in the leading role. The play in 1923 was taken to New York City and put on for the benefit of Life's Fresh Air Fund." She recalls the audience to be "a most sophisticated one who marvelled at our temerity in such an undertaking."

Regrettably, according to David Little, he did not inherit the thespian talents of his father, Harry, who was a former member of the Concord Dramatic Club and a president of the Players. But from where he sat in the audience, the continued appreciation of their work has been strong over the years. "Theatre is magic wherever it is performed. Spending several eve-

The Concord Players perform *Clarence*. Tennis
star, Bill Tilden, seated on the sofa, played the
leading role. 1923. (Courtesy of the Concord
Free Public Library)

LYCEUM THEATRE
Sunday Evening, May 13th
8:20 o'clock

WILLIAM T. TILDEN II
IN
CLARENCE
By Booth Tarkington
Supported by the CONCORD PLAYERS
Directed by SAMUEL MERWIN
For the benefit of LIFE'S FRESH AIR FUND

Seats at $3.00, $2.00 and $1.00
now on sale at
Tyson's, McBride's and Hotel Algonquin

or by application to Life, 598 Madison Ave., New York City

The Concord Players went to New York City
for a benefit performance of *Clarence* in 1923.
(Courtesy of the Concord Free Public Library)

nings a year at performances by the
Concord Players gave many Concordians
their chief exposure to live theatre during
the 1920s and 1930s.

"Conveniently located in the Veterans
Building, the Players offered for our entertainment venerable turkeys of the reper-
tory stage, Shakespeare, and excellent

plays which had graced Broadway only a
few years before. A good comedy sold the
most tickets and kept the Players solvent,
but the memory of serious plays convinc-
ingly performed sticks in my mind. My
spine always tingles with anticipation
when the curtain goes up. And when it
went down at the end of a performance in
the old days, the audience was invited
backstage to see how some of the magic
was created. I loved that!"

The Debut of *Little Women:* A Concord Players Tradition

The recent 150th anniversary of Louisa
May Alcott's birth was an occasion to celebrate the tradition begun by the Concord
Players in 1932, when they commemo-
rated her centennial. Since 1932, the play
Little Women has been performed every
ten years, with the exception of the wartime period in 1942. There is a sense of
continuity as members of the production
from past decades return again. By developing the tradition of performing *Little
Women,* the Concord Players seek to keep
alive Louisa May Alcott's love for performing in plays, that were first put on at her
home and later for the people of the town.

Back in 1932, when preparations were
being made for the author's centennial
birthday celebration, Marian Miller remembers that the proposal to dramatize

The first production of *Little Women* in 1932 by the Concord Players. Seated in center is Louisa Alcott Kussin as Meg; kneeling is Cornelia Lunt as Beth; and standing, Caroline Farnsworth as Jo, and Molly Harlow as Amy. (Courtesy of the Concord Players)

Alcott's most famous book received divided support among the directors of the Players. Her husband Hans was serving on the board at the time and was a strong advocate of the idea, and ultimately there was agreement to give it a try. In that first production, Hans Miller played the part of

Professor Bhaer, while Marian created the costumes and did the makeup. She tried to bring enough period authenticity to the costumes without distracting from the story itself. "If this play had been costumed absolutely accurately according to the period, much of it would have seemed extreme and would have diverted attention from the story itself. It is for the costumer to advance, not hinder, the action of the play and to so modify the styles of a bygone time that they appear natural."

A special feature of that first production was the casting of Louisa Alcott "Polly" Kussin in the role of her grandmother, Meg, and her brother, Bronson Alcott Pratt, in the part of his great-grandfather, Mr. March. Kussin remembers that "it was plain good fun. We had a wonderful time together and we even took our performances to Lexington and Cambridge, which was very unusual for those days."

In fact, after their four performances in Concord, two in Lexington, and one in Cambridge, the Players had reached an audience of 3,550. For three of the performances, all tickets were sold and "people had to be refused admission," read the local newspaper accounts. "The Players had to refuse no less than sixteen offers from organizations, which were ready and able to assume the responsibilities of backing the production. One offer came from as far away as Rosemont, Pennsylvania."

Marian Miller was a writer for the *Concord Journal* at the time and remembers the drama critic, Walter Prichard Eaton, from the *New York Herald-Tribune,* attending a performance. His review was "eagerly awaited" and the Players were not disappointed. In his article for the *Tribune,* Eaton describes purchasing tickets at Richardson's drugstore, and the conversation that followed.

" 'Better get there early,' said the clerk. 'Seems to be a rush and no seats reserved. Don't know why. Generally the Players don't nearly sell out on the opening night.'

" 'Perhaps it is because the play is *Little Women*,' we suggested.

" 'Maybe,' said the clerk. 'There are two Alcotts in the cast and they say people are coming from as far as New Bedford.'

" 'Here are two who have come farther than that,' we replied and went to find a room at the Inn."

Eaton praised the Concord Players as "one of the best amateur groups in New England. They gave an excellent performance. The audiences were drawn so largely from outside the town that the usual amateur family party effect was absent and the play, once it had begun, stood or fell on its merits."

Standing in awe of the whole proceedings that year was fifteen-year-old Heddie Root (Kent). Serving as an usher with her sister, Anne, she was already smitten with her lifelong passion for the theatre. "From the age of nine, I would accompany my uncle, Ripley Gage, and my parents to 51 Walden, which they called The Hall. My uncle Ripley loved performing and for that first production played the part of Mr.

Laurence. My mother, Olive, was on the costume committee and my father, George, whistled the part of Beth's robin."

Though other towns honored the author's one hundredth birthday with exercises and performances, Eaton remarked, "There can be no other performances with quite the air of those in Concord." And in a letter written to Hans Miller, Eaton expressed his amazement at the production's "high standard, higher than I have seen in any other New England amateur group, and the continued popularity of Miss Alcott. The Newark Library tells me, they have 159 copies of *Little Women* and often all of them are out. You must feel well repaid for your labors. There's life in the old theatre yet when it has something to offer and knows how to offer it."

"Waltz Me Around Again Willie"

Oh, waltz me around again, Willie,
Around, around, around
And life is all dreamy
As peaches and creamy,
Oh, don't let my feet touch the ground.

(Played to the tempo of the hurdy-gurdy)

When the century wore a younger face, entertainment was found close to home, and the evening's fun and the haircut and shoeshine that were part of getting ready fitted the budget with ease.

STATE ARMORY CONCORD

SATURDAY, DEC. 8, 1917 at 8.15   ADMISSION 20c.

MARY PICKFORD
IN
REBECCA OF
SUNNYBROOK FARM

FROM THE PLAY BY KATE DOUGLAS WIGGIN AND CHARLOTTE THOMPSON
SCENARIO BY FRANCIS MARION   DIRECTED BY MARSHALL NEILAN
PRESENTED BY
ARTCRAFT PICTURES
CORPORATION

The movies were popular attractions shown locally at the Veterans Building on Walden Street and in West Concord at the Association Hall on Commonwealth Avenue. Poster 1917. (Courtesy of Nancy Dee)

The West Concord Shoe Store would be open late Friday and Saturday nights, crowded with men waiting for a ten-cent shoeshine, remembers Joe Hay, whose father, Carl, opened the store in 1900. Often the men, he says, would drop in before going on to one of the local dances, either at the old Association Hall on Commonwealth Avenue or the Exchange Hall in South Acton. "As a youth that's how I got my spending money for the movies."

While the Association Hall would be cleared for dances on a Saturday night, earlier in the day, movies would be shown there and Hay recalls "the mood music" that Marion Fredericks played through all the silent movies. Charlie Comeau managed the movies there for Benjamin Derby, the postmaster in West Concord, whom he worked for while attending college. "Managing the movies was quite an experience. Tickets cost eleven cents downstairs, seventeen cents upstairs."

While the movies were silent, the movie theatre took on an entertainment comedy of its own," laughs Comeau as he describes the helmet-like hats the policemen, hired to keep order, wore at the time. "After intermission, when I sold enough peanuts, the boys would bounce these off the policeman's hat, and if they were caught, they were thrown out. Sometimes there was a soloist performing as well, whose talent left a lot to be desired."

On the other side of town, Anna Manion was one of the regulars at the silent movies, "every Saturday afternoon or evening, depending on our age, at the Veterans Building, now 51 Walden. There was the familiar serial, like *Perils of Pauline,* followed by the regular movie. And there was always a piano player to entertain us before, during, and after the movie."

A solid line of customers, waiting their turn on Saturdays for haircuts and a shave, was a familiar sight at the barbershop, where the customers in town were known by name. Conversation and the sharing of local news came with the popular "shave and a haircut, two bits" during the 1920s and 1930s, and the barbershop was the congenial gathering spot.

Many can still recall the tingling sensation of hot towels placed over their faces to soften the beard and at the end of the shave to open up the pores. "The key was keeping the blade sharp," explains barber David Palmucci, who continues the family business in Concord that was started by his father Joseph. "Customers were understanding though and tolerated the rash or nick that sometimes went with the shave." But shaves, adds Palmucci, began to die out in the 1950s when the safety edge razor by Gillette came into widespread use, and since have become a luxury service usually found at hotels.

Local minstrel shows were a popular form of entertainment put on by the Knights of Columbus which took place at Monument Hall. "A minstrel show had all kinds of acts, people sang and danced, and through it all there was a great deal of merriment," relates Jim Powers. "A con-

tinuous line of jokes were generated to a large extent by what we called end men, who were white men with their faces blackened. I was an end man many times and so were Terry and John McHugh and Tommy Tombeno. We told simple little jokes which at the time were appreciated and enjoyed, but today you would laugh at them for their simplicity."

"One end man would call out," says Terry McHugh, 'what are those two suitcases doing out in the aisle?' and another would answer, 'those are no suitcases, they're George Clark's feet.' And George would double over with laughter." A highlight of any of the minstrel shows, he adds, were the topical songs, which poked fun at people and events. And people laughed easily at ethnic humor, says Powers, about themselves and others, and knew no offense was meant. The end of the minstrel shows came in the 1950s, when this form of entertainment, with its origins in the South, no longer seemed to belong at a time of increasing civil rights awareness, as white men found it no longer respectful to blacken their faces.

A keg of beer in the cellar and some wine, the music of a violin and accordian, and a gathering at a neighbor's house was all that was needed to have a good old "kitchen racket," explains Powers. From the family's home on Grant Street, he would watch the neighbors gather for the Saturday night dancing. "The first thing the men would do was to pick up the stove and take it outside to make room for the

Fast stepping and spirited times during a minstrel show at Monument Hall. Left to right:
Tom Tombeno, Lib Hayes, Terry McHugh,
Eleanor Byron, Jim Powers, Margaret Sheehan
Crosby, Joe McGann, Mary Hennessey. (Collection of the Concord Historical Commission,
courtesy of Jim Powers)

119   When Entertainment Was Close to Home

A 1925 minstrel show put on by the Knights of
Columbus. This popular form of entertainment
included a variety of musical and comedy acts
performed by local residents. (Collection of the
Concord Historical Commission, courtesy of
Terry McHugh)

General Studios 109 Stuart St., Boston.

121   When Entertainment Was Close to Home

dancing, which was largely jigs and reels. It was a great lively time, though there was always some question about whether the kitchen floor itself would hold up. So often a pole or post would be used to prop the floor up from the basement. I remember that being done in our house and it is probably there to this day."

Above all Powers would love once again to be able to stand back in a corner and see the dancers going by, and just one more time hear "the off-key voice of some old codger singing:

Shake hands with your uncle Mike 'me boy,
Shake hands with your cousin Kate
And here is the girl you used to swing down on the garden gate.
Shake hands with all the neighbors and kiss the colleens all,
You're as welcome now as the flowers in May to dear old Donegal."

14

Concord's Social Circle

"Perhaps it is because we have done nothing at all as a body, that we have lasted this long," says David Little, a long-time member of the Social Circle in Concord. Little is the eighth generation in a line of Barretts to belong to this unique organization whose very origins parallel the formation of our nation.

"It started out in 1782, because a group of men had been members of the Committee of Correspondence, men who had been planning and plotting Concord's part in the American Revolution and had so much fun getting together without their wives, that when the war was over, they had no more excuse to go out in the evening. So they invented one and they put together the Social Circle in Concord."

The stated purpose at its founding was "to strengthen the social affections and disseminate useful communications among its members." The membership has stayed constant at twenty-five and, relates Little, has traditionally included "several selectmen, the town moderator, the minister of the First Parish Church, a doctor, and lawyer, and this continues to today. But with the growth of the town's population, it is obvious that we cannot be representative of the town or very influential in its decisions."

Roger Fenn explains that there is no formal structure to their body other than a host for the evening meeting and a secretary-treasurer. Fourteen meetings are held, twice a month on Tuesday evenings for the year, beginning in October. "It has been remarkably steady in keeping the same routine since 1782 and remains a very useful group that has no organized influence in town government." "Most of the members of the Social Circle have served the town in one capacity or another, so they are interested in what is of importance to the town," says Bert Newbury. "There is no sinister backroom decision making. It is strictly a social organization and it is up to the host for the evening to decide what form the discussion will take."

"The Social Circle has never decided anything as an organized body," adds Little. "They have never gotten up and said the Circle suggests, demands, or requires that the town do this or that. But it has been a very good place for two political opponents, shall we say, coping with some major issue in town that was being debated with more heat than light, to sit down at dinner with a drink in your hand and say, 'Hey George, you really are loose in the flue on this issue. Now the way I see it is thus and so,' and these things could be reasoned out calmly and no face lost and no great triumphs made before a big audience. It is useful for that purpose, very useful."

It was during the middle of the nineteenth century that the practice began of writing biographical memoirs of deceased members which have since reached six volumes of publication. The most widely known member of Concord's Social Circle has been Ralph Waldo Emerson, elected in 1839 and a member for forty-three years.

Emerson wrote to a Boston friend in 1844, "Much the best society I have ever known is a club in Concord called the Social Circle, consisting always of twenty-five of our citizens, doctor, lawyer, farmer, trader, miller, mechanic, etc., solidest of men, who yield the solidest of gossip. Harvard University is a wafer compared to the solid land which my friends represent. I do not like to be absent from home on Tuesday evenings in winter." The last meeting that Emerson attended was the celebration of the Social Circle's 100th anniversary, held one month before he died on April 27. And in 1982 in his honor, Social Circle members chose to postpone their bicentennial celebration until after the centennial commemoration of Emerson's death.

Prohibition was the order of the day fifty years ago when the Social Circle marked its 150th anniversary and toasts were made in the figurative sense only. One of the speakers that evening, local historian Allen French, aptly appraised the group's continued significance. "I question if any town, anywhere, has such a valuable record of the lives of average citizens. It is a procession of men in sober, everyday clothes, living common-place lives, from whose tales can be drawn valuable lessons. We see a series of pictures of the streets and houses of the old Town, in which move the men into whose lives we are looking."

Yet French finds the record of his companions "not so very average either," for they "strongly influenced the thought and action of the town. One cannot but marvel at the amount of public work done in a town like Concord, at great cost of time, in furthering the general activities. Our memories are pictures of life and studies of how it has been lived. In the lives of individual members, as interwoven with that of the Town, there is much to be learned . . ."

15
Country Doctors

A country town had its country doctors—
they were there before the age of special-
ists and medical centers, treating a wide
range of ailments and making house-
calls regardless of weather. Stories of Dr.
George E. Titcomb (1854–1923) and Dr.
Isaiah Lovell Pickard (1866–1947), for example, show their individualistic bent and
colorful personalities and have now passed
on into town lore.

"Dr. Titcomb was one of the greatest
doctors we ever had," recalls Gertrude
Hagerty. "He lived on Sudbury Road and
when you called him, it seemed before you
had the phone hung up, he would be at the
house. In the winter he went by horse and
sleigh, but when the drifts were too high
and the roads unplowed, he would take the
horse out of the sleigh, get on its back and
finish his calls. Movies used to be in the
armory on Everett Street and when Dr.
Titcomb would go to the movies Saturday
night, invariably a message would come
for him that he would have to go back to
his office. I don't think he ever got to see a
movie through."

Anna Manion's mother was a nurse who
used to assist Dr. Titcomb when he delivered babies at home. "She also etherized
the patients when he was taking their appendix out on a scrubbed kitchen table."

People joked that the doctor couldn't be allowed into the library for fear he would
take the appendix out of the books.

Velina Bregoli tells of the time her
father, Ruggiero, resisted the ether on
the operating table, grabbed his clothes,
and bolted home with the doctor catching
up with him but unable to persuade him to
return. "My father years later died at age
sixty-eight with his appendix still in, but
he and the doctor were friends nevertheless. My father told us the story when he
was walking home from work on Baker
Bridge just beyond Lake Walden, after a
snowstorm with a shovel in his hand to
clear the way, when Dr. Titcomb came
from behind in his horse and sleigh. The
drifts were too big for him to get through.
My father told him to abandon the wagon,
and he shoveled a path for the two of them
to walk home. The horse, having been sent
on ahead, was in the barn when they
returned."

Jim Powers remembers Dr. Titcomb
driving like a madman through the snow
en route to his calls. "Sometimes he would
get Ed Haley to drive for him. They would
have a big bear rug over their knees and
he was with the doctor when they made
too wide a turn coming around the corner
of Snow's Pharmacy and tipped over."

Dr. Titcomb's brusque manner is illus-
trated by the story about the time when he
was asked to apologize for his rudeness to
an operator of the phone company, then located above Snow's Pharmacy. "Are you
the lady I told to go to hell the other day?"

Dr. George Titcomb. Circa 1900. (Courtesy of the Concord Free Public Library)

the doctor inquired, only to add, "Well, you needn't bother!"

In West Concord, residents of Concord Junction speak of the indomitable Dr. Pickard of Highland Street for whom Old Pickard Road is named. "My father was a doctor during the horse and buggy days," says his daughter, Elizabeth, "Lib," one of the doctor's eight children. "He was trained at Harvard and they have many of his medical papers and equipment. He kept three horses in the barn and his black bag was always ready and filled with instruments. And if you wanted, he would even pull your teeth. My father remained a farmer all his life, surrounded by his cows, horses, and chickens. He would rise

at 5:30 in the morning to go out to the woodpile and feed the furnace. And as often as not he would come into the house singing away—it didn't matter that it was on just one note or that he couldn't carry a tune, he just loved music."

A longtime neighbor of the doctor, who lived next door to him on Highland Street, was Joseph Hay. "Dr. Pickard was a typical hearty fellow," he remembers. "The sort who would stand on the front porch and say, 'It's going to be a fine day.' He

Dr. Isaiah Pickard. Circa 1945. (Collection of the Concord Historical Commission, courtesy of the Pickard family)

owned farmland in Sudbury and sold milk before pasteurization. He said, after all, that milk is milk. As our next-door neighbor, I would see him giving haircuts on the porch with horse clippers and a bowl or making ice cream. I would help him break the ice up with a hammer and my reward was licking the blades."

When the horse and buggy gave way to the motor car, Hay remembers the Model T Ford that the doctor kept in the barn in the rear of his house. "He also bought a Hudson and the first Cadillac. It had two cylinders and looked like a buggy without a horse in the front, but he seemed to prefer the Model T. There was an old surrey with a fringe on top as well, and I got to drive the horse. Dr. Pickard was an excellent diagnostician, and when you called him, he'd come. There was plenty of whooping cough, measles, and scarlet fever that required patients to be quarantined. And he would even pull your teeth if needed by wrapping a bag around blacksmith pliers."

"Tuberculosis, pneumonia, and the flu were major concerns then," comments Lib. "The flu epidemic in 1918 hit nearby Fort Devens especially bad. Row upon row of coffins were laid out, so many had died. The flu took the life of my sister during her first year of teaching in New Hampshire." Florence Damon remembered the special sadness of the doctor, who having treated so many locally during the epidemic, was out of reach of his own daughter and couldn't save her.

An easy bedside manner came naturally to Dr. Theodore Chamberlin, who arrived at age thirty to practice medicine in Concord in 1898. "He came at the invitation of Dr. Edward Emerson, the son of Ralph Waldo Emerson, who was about to retire," says Chamberlin's daughter, Anne Newbury. He personified to those who remember him, the old-time family doctor, going about town with a horse and buggy, and when it snowed, a sleigh. He lived at first in the old block house on Main Street,

Dr. Theodore Chamberlin. Circa 1925. (Collection of the Concord Historical Commission, courtesy of Anne Chamberlin Newbury)

where he had his office, and which has since been moved to Lowell Road. In 1905 the family home became the white painted brick house on Lowell Road, which had been the home of Dr. Josiah Bartlett, and which Chamberlin had enlarged to accommodate a growing family that would include eight children. "There was no hospital in Concord at the time," says Newbury, "so all the medical work, even surgery, was done in people's homes or in the doctor's office."

At the time of Chamberlin's arrival, there were many local cases of malaria, which were frequently blamed on the newly arrived Italian immigrants working on town sewer systems. But Chamberlin, in listing the cases of malaria for the state board of health, found that most of these cases occurred in homes that were poorly screened. And working with Dr. Theobald Smith, an authority on malaria, they collected mosquitoes in the swamps and low areas of town and promoted the understanding that the disease was spread in this manner.

Beyond his private practice, Chamberlin was a physician for the reformatory, supervising the construction of a hospital there, built with prison labor; and when the Middlesex School opened in 1901, he served as the physician there for a decade. Though retiring from private practice in 1910, he continued to have an interest in medical care. An admirer of Dr. Walter Fernald, he served as a member of the corporation and a trustee for the school then

called the Massachusetts School for the Feeble Minded.

Interested in seeing a hospital established in Concord, Chamberlin was a member of the committee that coordinated the building of Emerson Hospital through the generosity of his friend, Charles Emerson, the nephew of the poet. Emerson had been grateful for the care that his wife had received at the Boston Deaconess Hospital during her last illness in the early months of 1911 and donated 100 acres of land, overlooking the Sudbury River on the Old Road to Nine Acre Corner, that included $20,000 for the building of a hospital to be administered by the New England Deaconess Association. The hospital opened its doors in November 1911 with fourteen beds and thirteen years later was deeded from the Association to a corporation of interested citizens within the town. Dr. Chamberlin upon his death in 1939 left money to the Deaconess Association in memory of his father, Seth Chamberlin, to be used as a Home for Aged Men and Couples, now part of the present Deaconess retirement home complex.

The Romance of Veterinary Medicine

"There was a certain romance to veterinary medicine when I began practicing that seems to be gone today," says Dr. Edgar "Brud" Tucker. "The veterinarian was the one important individual between

Emerson Hospital when it was the Deaconess
Hospital. Circa 1920. (Courtesy of Emerson Hospital)

Early operating room at Emerson Hospital.
Circa 1925.(Courtesy of Emerson Hospital)

Dr. Edgar Tucker. Circa 1942. (Collection of the Concord Historical Commission, courtesy of Dr. Edgar Tucker)

success and failure for the farmer dependent on his animals for a livelihood. We exercised our ingenuity to solve problems, getting through the roads on a snowy day to help deliver a calf, performing a caesarean by lantern light, or getting a horse out of the barn cellar because the barn floor had broken. Veterinary medicine has so completely changed during the last twenty-five to thirty years that most peo-

ple can't comprehend what we had to go through prior to World War II."

It was June 1941 when Tucker got off the train in Concord, "green as grass" from Cornell Veterinary College to be an assistant to Dr. Alden Russell, the only veterinarian in town from 1923 until 1936. Russell's home was at 75 Elm Street, where he had an office for the treatment of small animals and "where we made our own medicines" until the Concord Animal Hospital was built in 1953, says Tucker. "We had certain few drugs and used them for darn near everything we saw."

The town had many farms when Tucker arrived and the open land was considerable. "I came principally as a cow man, and the troubles that individual cows could get into were out of this world. There were 400 cows on Virginia Road alone, Gordon Hutchins's Punkatasset farm on Monument Street had 110 head of cows and two teams of big heavy draft horses, and the prison had an active farming operation of 18 horses, 150 cows, 5,000 to 6,000 chickens, and 600 to 800 pigs. So many of the family farms had a cow in the backyard. People were used to living with them and there was a strong bond of personal affection between the owner and his animal."

Many people, Russell says, used to suffer from malarial or undulant fever, a fluctuating fever which was contracted by drinking the milk of infected cows. Similarly, bovine tuberculosis was contracted by drinking the milk of tubercular cows. "The method of control was to test the cattle and slaughter those that were diseased. Milk pasteurization, introduced in the 1920s, significantly reduced the problem, but most of my generation was exposed to tuberculosis." Tucker adds that the bovine strain of tuberculosis affected the bones and joints and was what caused so many hunchbacks and problems of the spine and thorax region, while the human strain was called consumption and affected the lungs.

When spraying took place locally, says Tucker, cows often fell victim. "Hutchins lost twenty-eight yearling heifers one year to lead poisoning when his apple trees were sprayed, and the spray reached the grass and leaves. Animals are affected by small amounts of lead to a greater degree than humans. And when the town sprayed for poison ivy, that spread right onto Eddie Carlson's pasture on Virginia Road and affected his large herd." A lot of epsom salts were used as laxatives, he says, as a help in treating lead poisoning of cattle and horses.

There were fewer riding horses then and more farm work horses, observes Russell. "Black water disease in horses, caused by heavy feeding when idle, was almost always fatal. In the 1930s this was found to be curable by injections of calcium in the vein." Encephalus myalitis, carried by mosquitoes, occurred sporadically for years, but in 1938 became epidemic, according to Russell. He remembers the year

well, because of the great hurricane that occurred and the difficulty he had getting home. "We were all vaccinating horses against the disease and I was out in Bedford when the hurricane struck. Trees were blown down, roads blocked, and I had to leave my car and walk two miles to Bedford Center. I got the last bus to Arlington Heights and then a taxi was able to get me home from Route 2 which had just been completed and was one road wide enough not to be blocked by fallen trees."

Piggeries were plentiful locally, says Tucker, with large ones owned by Carl Anderson along Virginia Road and by Lorenzo Ruggiero in what is now Wright Road and his brother Patrick in what is now the Deacon Haynes Road area. He remembers only too well his close calls when chased by a sow. "Sows can be terrifying. Nothing compares to an ugly sow weighing between 400 and 500 pounds, looking to take a bite out of you. When disease hit pigs it spread throughout the herd. This was true of hog cholera. All pigs who were garbage fed then were vulnerable to this virus, a lethal and constant threat. We vaccinated them shortly after they were weaned and I remember one day we vaccinated 2,000 pigs and wore out nine men doing it. By the early 1970s the vaccine was no longer used and any outbreaks were controlled by quarantine and slaughter. Today hog cholera has finally been eliminated in this country, a major accomplishment."

But the explosion in medical knowledge aside, Tucker has more than a wistful longing for the days "when we vets were tied to the mainstay of the farmer's livelihood and to the economy. We were the important guys that had to get out, bucking the snowdrifts, working in the broiling sun, or sewing up a horse by moonlight. There was a heightened feeling of essentiality about our lives that made for the drama and romance of the practicing vet."

16
Farming the Land

Concord Grass Was the Finest

Spring planting meant a variety of market garden crops but none was more important in Concord than asparagus and strawberries during the early part of the century.

All the land that held its moisture through June was used for strawberries, while the sandy fields for miles around were covered with asparagus, says Laurence Richardson. "Concord raised more asparagus than any other town in the area and 'Concord Grass' was a standard of excellence."

"With asparagus you got cash in the spring early," remarks Terry McHugh, who farmed with his brothers along Lexington and Old Bedford roads. Within Concord, explains Antonino Scimone of Bedford Street, there was a good combination of high and low lands, with the high land particularly suitable for raising asparagus. Asparagus, he says, was such an important crop locally that the government set up an experimental station on the Charles Prescott land on Bedford Street to determine the cause and treatment of disease affecting the asparagus.

Asparagus rust was the cause of significant damage to Ralph Hemenway's father's crop. "My dad in 1898 bought what was then one of the better asparagus farms in Concord on Fairhaven Road. But what he didn't know was that asparagus rust had struck the roots killing them all. The whole field had to be replanted, and since it takes three years for the asparagus to bear commercially, he had quite a rough time of it and had to sell part of the farm to keep a roof over our heads."

As a young boy Hemenway learned how to cut and bunch asparagus. "The cutter would have to stoop over and cut the spear about two inches below the ground. You had to be careful not to cut the new shoots coming up around it. After cutting, the spears were brought into the shed to be bunched. A buncher was a flat piece of wood about two inches thick and the center would be hollowed a bit to lay the string to tie each bunch of asparagus. Each bunch was made up of spears of uniform size. Then it would be taken to another table that had a cutter like a paper cutter, and each bunch was cut on the bottom to even up the spears so they would be of the same size and height."

Hemenway remembers that several men came with trucks to the farms every evening to pick up the asparagus that had been cut during the day. "The truckers would take the produce, including other vegetables, into Boston to the commission houses at Faneuil Hall market. The trucker would leave the name of each grower with the commission houses and the commissioners would sell the produce and pay the farmer the selling price less their commission. There were times when the farmer didn't get anything at all from the sale.

"When we went by horse and wagon to the market we would leave around noontime to get there by dark and stay overnight. The loaded wagon would be left in the street, the horse taken to a stable, and we would return to sleep in the hayloft."

Bunching asparagus meant a promotion, compared to picking strawberries, says Anna Manion. "At least I could sit down in the shed to bunch asparagus with the older women. You felt quite grown up if you had gone past the strawberry picking stage. All the boys started cutting asparagus at 5:30 in the morning before going to school. In strawberry season, we all picked strawberries for the local neighborhood farmers at two cents a box. I never liked doing it but the whole gang was there so I went along. I probably was one of the slowest pickers and got the lowest pay."

Sanfred Benson remembers getting three dollars a bushel for asparagus, with three dozen bunches packed to a bushel box, and eight to ten cents a quart for strawberries, with thirty-two quarts packed to the crate. Of the two, Benson preferred to handle the asparagus which grew well in the light, sandy soil. "If the asparagus froze, you didn't necessarily lose it the way you did with strawberries." "Everybody that had a piece of land around here grew asparagus," adds McHugh.

A well known Concord collector of Indian relics, Benjamin Lincoln Smith, found the dominance of early-twentieth-century asparagus growing tough competition for the archaeologist. "The deep plowing necessary for asparagus growing resulted in the soil being turned upside down and partially destroyed a good many sites particularly along the borders of the rivers. The Indian relics stayed on the surface and when cutting the stalks, the farmers were practically looking at the relics." The building of homes similarly upset a great many sites. Smith was able to find most of his collection on the soil surface following rainstorms and after the spring and fall plowing. "By 1910 when I began looking, the larger more spectacular relics had been picked up by asparagus cutters for the past twenty to thirty years and they were the start of collections for various families."

The Days of the Milkman and the Nickel Cone

Not so long ago, it would have been inconceivable to pay more than fifteen cents for an ice cream soda, ten cents for a milkshake, or twenty cents for a frappe. Far from being prices of another century, they were what people readily remember from the 1940s before the inflation spiral began.

Floyd Verrill was an active dairy farmer in Concord then and by 1938 was selling 1,000 quarts of milk a day, while a future state senator from Lincoln, Jim DeNormandie, was selling 500 quarts daily. Deciding to form a partnership, they bought land on the corner of Sudbury Road and Thoreau Street, which was a vacant lot then with a path leading to the depot. In 1939 the Dairy was opened featuring the latest milk processing equipment and an ice cream parlor. Two years later a locker plant was added, which Verrill explains flourished until private freezers were available for use. "At the height of our business we were selling 12,000 quarts of milk daily including servicing two hospitals and delivering two trucks of forty-quart jugs to Harvard College. And with twenty-two dealers delivering milk in Concord at one time, competition was strong."

When Floyd and his wife Amy arrived in Concord in 1922 and bought the Carrigan farm on Sudbury Road, most farmers had two or three cows for their own use and a number of people had family cows. A few farmers had small milk routes, but with laws requiring pasteurization, most farmers went out of the retail milk business and local people like Verrill and Fred Jones took over their routes. Verrill charted his course as a dairy farmer by buying a herd of thirty cows and a milk route in Lexington. Milk was retailing for fourteen cents a quart then and a farm laborer was receiving forty dollars per month with room and board.

As business grew Verrill enlarged his facilities. In 1927 he bought the Prime farm at Nine Acre Corner, which originally belonged to Rodney Wheeler, and purchased a herd of sixty cows. "The milk was put into forty-quart jugs, set into a refrigerator tank of water and then taken to the other farm for processing. At first we took the milk from the cows and ran it over a tubular cooler with cold water running through it. It was then bottled with a machine that did four bottles at a time. Finally, it was iced and put in the cooler." Later Verrill built a new milk room, installed refrigeration, a continuous rotary bottling machine, and a pasteurizer. "I think I was the first to start pasteurizing in Concord and I was the first to put milk in the schools. We tried to get as much milk as possible delivered before breakfast. Late risers sometimes were troubled with sour milk in hot weather and frozen milk popping up an inch or two out of the bottles in cold weather. It was not until after we built the dairy that we put out insulated boxes."

Verrill explains that people then would look at the cream line to judge a good quart of milk. Bottles were made with long slim necks to make the cream line look deeper. Later when milk was homogenized, such merchandising no longer was necessary and bottles began to appear with short thick necks. As milkman, Verrill was often the first person on the roads and his truck led the way on snowy mornings. "One winter there was a week when there was so much snow we weren't able to use a truck and had to use sleds pulled by a team of horses to get through to Lexington. Towards spring there were deep ice ruts in the road so it was necessary to carry an axe in order to get out."

The milk delivery business declined during the 1960s, says Verrill. "Rising costs had made it necessary for me to reduce deliveries to three times weekly and 1968 was our last year of operation. I used to say anyway that a dairy farmer never could count on what he could make for the year, only what he could lose." Verrill's son Steve manages the farm today but only a small quantity of milk is delivered in town and that by outside dealers. The early rising milkman has gone the way of the nickel cone and the twenty-cent sundae.

Farming Nine Acre Corner

By the time Russell "Rusty" Wheeler was ready to go into farming, as nine generations of Wheelers had before him, his father advised against it. It was increasingly difficult to make a living from the family farm and it represented the end of an era for a small corner of Concord that had once been dominated by members of the Wheeler family.

Rusty's home was the "plains" area of Nine Acre Corner, which included Powder Mill and Plainfield roads and roads that would subsequently bear the names of his grandfather, father, and uncle—Anson, Raymond, and Alden roads, when the family farm was sold for house lots in 1963.

The family farm was basically a truck farm consisting of 130 acres where the crops were rotated regularly, he says. "We felt fortunate to have both high and low lands to farm. If the lowlands were too wet, they could use the highlands and vice versa." As many as twenty-five men were employed year round. The many greenhouses that the Wheelers owned could keep these men working through the winter, and labor intensive farming practices prevailed until the early 1920s when the cost of operating a farm increased to the point where mechanization was introduced.

His grandfather Anson, says Rusty, was the first to build a greenhouse in Middlesex County and the first to grow cucumbers under glass. Anson's prize greenhouse crop was rhubarb grown in a specially constructed greenhouse where the top could be removed. A layer of snow was allowed to fall on the rhubarb, giving it its winter season and then the rhubarb would be forced under glass. "Before spring would come, the rhubarb would taste tremendous and sweet and was such in demand in the cities that we could afford to ship it by railway express to New York and Chicago. Often ships like the *Queen Mary* would buy a whole load before leaving from Boston."

He remembers his Uncle Alden loving farming so much "that he would seem to stand there at times, watching the crops grow." His father Raymond was more of a tinkerer with equipment. "He never

The Wheeler farm at Nine Acre Corner, boyhood home of Raymond Wheeler. Circa 1900.
(Collection of the Concord Historical Commission, courtesy of Rusty and Marian Wheeler)

Alden Wheeler on his 1920 Moline tractor.
Circa 1927. (Collection of the Concord Histori-
cal Commission, courtesy of Rusty and Marian
Wheeler)

Raymond Wheeler loads the vegetable washer
that he invented. Circa 1935. (Collection of the
Concord Historical Commission, courtesy of
Rusty and Marian Wheeler)

bought anything new but would take the parts of trucks and anything else available for use. He put together a vegetable washing machine that could clean six to eight bushels of vegetables at once. He had the ingenuity to construct pipes and pumps and be one of the first farmers to irrigate the land, drawing water from nearby White Pond."

Though farmers, he explains, were too individualistic to form unions, the market gardeners of Middlesex County formed an association which used to meet every spring. "Every few years the association would meet at the Wheeler farm and have a good gabfest. Representatives from the Middlesex County Extension Service would be there to tell of the latest innovations in hybrid seed and fertilizer and advisors from other states would be giving talks as well. Because it was early spring when they met, the soil was muddy with a great many ruts, and fifteen to twenty cars would get stuck and require horses to pull them out. Because this seemed to happen with such regularity, a team of horses would already be standing there in anticipation."

His world of Nine Acre Corner was virtually a self-contained community with many of the families related through the Wheeler line to one another. There was even a Nine Acre Corner Improvement Association, which held regular meetings as well as social gatherings. Maude Ellis remembers these social gatherings when she and her family moved to their present Sud-

bury Road home, at the intersection of the Old Road to Nine Acre Corner, in 1928 from their Barrett's Mill Road home. "We had our own social life out here. I well remember the corn shucking parties at Esther Anderson's farm and sewing for Emerson Hospital at the Hallett house. The farms around us belonged to the Anderson, Brigham, and Wheeler families, who had been here for generations, and the more recent, Lufkin, Hallett, and Verrill families."

Her husband William was an entomologist with the Department of Agriculture, who had come to Concord to find a control for the corn borer and started his own insecticide business which provided many a boy in West Concord with after school employment. Their home, says Ellis, had formerly been the Green Apple Tea Room, which also sold antiques. "There is a box in our attic which confirms that," but the sparsely settled, little travelled Old Road to Nine Acre Corner then did not prove to be a good location for such a business to thrive, she adds.

During his boyhood, Rusty Wheeler saw his family's farm go from the horse-drawn wagon to several trucks hauling loads to Boston. "Delivery time to Boston by wagon took six to seven hours and could only carry half as much as the trucks, which could make the same trip in forty-five minutes. At the time of World War I, our family was already using trucks." Increased mechanization began to change the nature of farming that required a large amount of acreage to be cost efficient, and Rusty says his father saw what was coming. "He seemed to know that the day of the family farm was passing on."

Farming the East Quarter

"Call it dry farming," laughs Terry Mc-Hugh of the days before irrigation when all watering was done by hand. He lives in the farmhouse on Lexington Road, one of eleven children born there to Terence and Mary Dee McHugh. Both immigrants from Ireland, they purchased the home at a public auction, appropriately on St. Patrick's Day in 1880.

The McHughs farmed in the era of the horse-drawn plow and the spiked tooth harrow, spending considerable time walking behind the cultivator. Along with asparagus, strawberries were a big crop on the McHugh farm, whose major parcel was twenty acres of land on Old Bedford Road, now owned by the town. And with horse and wagon, family members took their turn on the ride to the Faneuil Hall market.

A number of the farms in the area, says McHugh, had fruit trees then: apple, pear, plum, cherry, and peach. While peaches were considered a risky crop due to the early frost, some farmers like his neighbor, George Clark, who lived on a stretch of land where Lexington Road meets the bypass of Routes 2 and 2A, raised a plentiful crop of peaches.

Many Irish farmers lived along Old Bedford and Virginia roads and included the Magurn, Dalton, Burke, Kenney, Mc-Manus, McGrath, McKenna, McCaffrey, Dolan, Cunningham, Fie, and Algeo families. They mixed easily, he says, with Yankee farmers like Ben and George Clark, and Frank Tuttle along Lexington Road, Caleb Wheeler on Virginia Road, and Swedish farmers Frank Peterson at the corner of Old Bedford Road and Virginia Road, and George Carlson on Virginia Road.

When the Kenney family came from Arlington in 1924 to Virginia Road, once called Virginia Flats and one of the town's first farmland, Lawrence Kenney remembers his father bringing with him a one-horse plow, a tip cart, manure wagon, a market wagon, a wheelbarrow, a cultivator, and two hoes. And like the Magurns, the Kenneys became big truck farmers in the East Quarter. During World War II, the Kenney farm was one of the area farms that used German prisoners-of-war labor from Fort Devens. "By seven in the morning," says Philip Kenney, "they would be working in the fields. I found them to be the best workers and we were friendly with one another." Former neighbor John Lambert, who had bought the old Peterson farmhouse in 1945, remembers seeing these prisoner-of-war farm laborers and their armed guards. "One time we saw quite a discussion going on and found that what was disturbing these German prisoners so much was the discarding of the

John McHugh. Circa 1970. (Collection of the
Concord Historical Commission)

Terry, Tom, and John McHugh on their Old
Bedford Road land. 1973. (Collection of the
Concord Historical Commission)

144   Farming the Land

poorer vegetables. They couldn't understand why good food was being thrown away."

The Scimone family was one of a number of Italian families who came from the region called Faro Superiore, Messina, and farmed along Bedford Street and Old Bedford Road. They included the Amendolia, Arena, Curro, Denaro, Inferrera, Marabello, Mazzeo, Rotondo, and Sorrenti families. Frank Scimone arrived in Concord in 1923, without his wife and a daughter, who were still in Italy, and like many other Italian farmers worked for the established farmers in the area to earn the money to bring the rest of the family over. After a time it was hoped that with sufficient earnings, land could be rented and finally purchased.

This ambition was realized for Scimone, who supplemented his income during the depression days of the 1930s by working as a mason. Eventually the Italian farmers were able to raise sufficient fruit and vegetables to set up roadside stands, which were lined with customers, describes his son Antonino. He and other family members run a lively business at their Old Bedford Road stand adjacent to the house their parents purchased, a reminder of the once active Italian farming community there. "These families were a close-knit commu-

Lawrence Kenney in fourteen acres of lettuce on Virginia Road, June 1949. (Collection of the Concord Historical Commission)

Grace and Frank Scimone at their Old Bedford Road farmstand. 1938. (Collection of the Concord Historical Commission, courtesy of the Scimone family)

nity making their own entertainment based on their Italian traditions. In the days when cars were still few and families could walk easily to one another's homes, it was common for four or five families to visit often with one another."

Before World War II and into the 1950s, he says, the active partnership between the small farmer and the federal government, through cost-sharing, kept the family farm going. "Any practice of the farmer to improve his land, such as liming and cover-cropping, was cost-shared with the government, at rates anywhere from 30 to 60 percent. And taxes were not as high as today. But in the early 1960s, things began to change, as cost-sharing declined, and with the increased demand for houses, farmland was sold as profitable houselots."

For Antonino Scimone there would be no memories of the earlier farming days were it not for the intervention of a local congresswoman in making his passage to America possible. While his mother and sister were able to join his father here in 1929, his own passage was blocked inexplicably within the bureaucracy of Benito Mussolini's government. The official reason given was that he had failed the physical because of eye problems. Yet his anxious grandparents with whom he remained were never told what this medical problem was nor how they could treat it, and Antonino's prospects for emigrating appeared bleak.

It was a standard procedure for area representatives to congratulate their constituents when they became U.S. citizens, he relates, and his father received such a letter from Congresswoman Edith Nourse Rogers with the closing paragraph that she would be available if he needed anything. "My father wrote to her about my being detained in Italy, not really expecting an answer." But the response did come and through her intervention with the American Consulate in Italy, he says, the redtape was cleared, "and my eyes were miraculously cured." The year was 1931 and for Antonino Scimone, *il mondo nuovo me a aspettava*— a new world was waiting.

17

The Immigrant Experience

by William M. Bailey

Native-Americans lived in the Concord area three to six thousand years ago. By the time of the English migration to Massachusetts Bay, however, there is little evidence of more than an occasional family living in Concord. Disease had taken the lives of most of the Native Americans in Massachusettts Bay on the eve of English colonization. Their presence was, nevertheless, felt by the English who settled in Concord in 1637, two years after receiving their charter. Their trails were used and extensive bartering occurred. The colonists' needs were often met by Native Americans who provided them with canoes, baskets, and other items.

Among Concord's English settlers were Peter and Grace Bulkeley, who came from Bedfordshire. Numerous English towns were represented in the first migration. Many of Concord's early settlers including the Bulkeleys left England for religious reasons, part of the great Puritan exodus, while others came for economic opportunity.

The first town record of blacks in Concord is the notation that "Antoner, ye son of Antoner and Margartt, both negroes,

was born April the 3rd, 1708." Six slaves were recorded in 1725. Of all the immigrants to Concord, only the slaves did not come to Concord by choice.

In 1835, two hundred years after Concord received its charter from the General Court, its population was still almost exclusively English in origin. A few inhabitants were Scottish. Twenty-eight blacks lived in Concord, enjoying the rather limited status of "freedmen." The town's population was soon to undergo a dramatic change.

During the 1840s, at the height of the Irish Potato Famine, Patrick and Maria Hagerty of County Roscommon came to Concord. According to family lore, he bought land on Sudbury Road near Conantum, where he sold sand for a dollar a wagonload to the Fitchburg Railroad, which came to Concord in 1846. Patrick Hagerty fought in the Civil War, leaving Maria and six children in Concord.

In 1872 Inga Voldmo left Loiten, Norway, for Concord, where she was to be employed as a servant for the Brooks family. Her sister Amalie and Helene Beckvold joined her shortly after. The following year, the minister of Loiten's Lutheran church stopped to visit the historic site of the Revolution on his way home from visiting friends and relatives in the Dakota territory. George Wheeler, a Sudbury Road farmer, told the minister that he would be happy to hire farm laborers from Norway, according to Alice Petersen. "Lars Petersen had to work for a whole year in Norway to buy a suit of clothes. He heard from the minister about the opportunity to work in Concord for George Wheeler. Mr. Wheeler paid the fare which was twenty-eight dollars, so he had to pay back that fare before he could earn any money in this country."

In 1893 Alessandro and Maria Macone, from Gaeta, a small town near Naples, Italy, bought a farm on Strawberry Hill. Their son John says, "My dad worshipped the soil. He raised zucchini squash, finocchi, basil, and Italian beans for the Boston market." So pungent was the smell of the basil in the late summer "that families from Boston, visiting their sons and husbands at the Concord Reformatory, would get the scent and follow it to their farm, asking to buy some for their cooking."

Charles and Adeline Pageau came to the United States from Quebec in 1880. At the turn of the century, they moved with their children to Concord. Charles and three of his sons, Aimee, George, and Leon, worked as carpenters for Isaac Beharrell, a West Concord contractor. Beharrell himself had emigrated to Concord in 1871 from Amherst, Nova Scotia.

The parents of Ida Jacobs Israel came to America from Lithuanian Russia. "I believe they came over around 1893 and my father, Samuel Jacobs, was a tailor; he did custom-made suits. I've since heard that Mr. McWalter, who had a shoe store on Main Street, was the one that suggested to my father to come to Concord, because he thought there was a need for a tailor."

All these residents of Concord—from the Native Americans on Nashawtuc Hill to Samuel and Ida Jacobs—were part of the great wave of immigrants who came here to live and labor. Studies of immigration to America usually exclude the Native Americans, the English colonists, and the slaves the English brought with them. With the exception of the Africans, however, their adventures and experiences were no different from those of the immigrants who followed them in the quest for survival and a new life. The nineteenth and twentieth centuries have witnessed massive voluntary migrations from Europe, and more recently Asia. Concord's experience has not been unlike that of other parts of Massachusetts, New England, and the United States.

Concord's image, however, is still that of a Yankee town, whose roots go back to England and to England alone. The town's history is, of course, responsible for this. Concord's rich colonial heritage, its renowned resistance to the British in April 1775, its central role (with Emerson, Thoreau, the Alcotts, and Hawthorne) in what Van Wyck Brooks called the literary "Flowering of New England," and its social hierarchy, which was, until quite recently, exclusively Yankee—each of these conditions has contributed to the image.

But there is another dimension to Concord's history, an examination of Concord's population after 1840 clearly shows. In the period just before and during the Civil War, a large Irish migration and an unusually high birth rate among the Irish combined to produce several years in which births to foreign-born Irish exceeded births to native-born Yankees. The 1910 United States Census lists Concord's population as 6,421 with a foreign-born population of 27 percent. Another 20 percent were second generation. Only 38 percent of Concord's population were of English origin. The Scandinavian name Olsen was the most common name in the 1925 Town Directory. Smith was second, Wheeler third, and Petersen/son (also Scandinavian) fourth. The same directory listed about one hundred families of Italian origin.

What opportunities were there in Concord for these immigrants? The industrial transformation that occurred here was not significantly different from that which occurred in other parts of the United States. Technology was intimately connected with the increase in immigration. The building of the railroad from Boston to Fitchburg in 1846 sustained the first significant migration of Irish to Concord. Italian laborers laid Concord's sewer system in 1898. The mills in West Concord—the powder mill, the Damon Woolen Mill, the Warner Pail Factory, the Allen Chair Company, the Boston Harness Company, and the Blueine Manufacturing Company—all demanded cheap and often highly skilled labor. Most of the laborers in these mills were not native-born Americans. Especially large numbers were from Canada, with significant contributions from Ireland, Scotland and England, and small numbers from at least a dozen other nations. Until World War I, on the other hand, the employees at the Concord Reformatory were largely of Yankee ancestry and came mostly from the New England states, especially Maine and New Hampshire. Status was associated with work at the prison.

Social and economic position, in addition to technology, affected immigration. As farms became more productive and the Boston market grew, it became essential to hire farm laborers. Many women on farms and in town came to expect maid servants. Hired help, in the period between the Civil War and World War I, was not necessarily a sign of wealth. After 1870 many Concord farmers employed at least one hired hand. As time went on, the larger farms had as many as a dozen laborers. Many of these farms could be found on Lexington and Old Bedford roads, on Lowell Road and Monument Street, and on the Old Road to Nine Acre Corner.

Most young Yankee men were not willing to work as farm laborers. Their sisters were equally averse to serving as domestics, and their parents discouraged them from accepting these positions. When suitable opportunities did not present themselves at home, many of these native sons and daughters were drawn to America's West. In spite of the large number of immigrants to Concord between 1850 and 1930, the town's population did not increase rapidly, because many Concordians were, like the European immigrants, striking out on their own and leaving for other parts.

The twenty-three domestics listed in Concord's 1860 census were all natives of Ireland. As the years went by, Irish settled in Concord in greater and greater numbers, working first on the established farms and for residents of Main Street and its arteries. Each town census underscores the mobility of the newcomers. As more and more Irish came to own farms, the ethnic composition of domestics and farm laborers changed, reflecting the patterns of migration to Concord. In 1870 a large number of Concord's hired help were from Nova Scotia, and by 1880 many Norwegians had joined them. In 1910 domestics came from a great number of foreign countries and many were second generation Americans, supplementing their parents' income or striking out on their own. By 1910 a new wave of immigrants had arrived: fifty Russian Poles were farm laborers; many Finnish women were domestics; and Italian gardeners worked on the larger Concord estates.

Concord's immigrant communities were continually recharged by new emigrants from the same region in the "Old Country." Perhaps as many as half of the Norwegians who came to Concord were from Loiten and surrounding towns in central Norway, not far from the Swedish border. More than a dozen Italian families who emigrated to Concord between 1912 and 1935 came from Faro Superiore, a small town on the island of Sicily, and its neigh-

boring villages. But Concord's largest immigrant group was not so localized— Concord's Irish came from every part of Ireland.

The Irish

The Potato Famine of the 1840s was a watershed in the history of human migration. Hundreds of thousands of Irish were forced to flee their homeland. Shiploads arrived weekly in Boston. The building of the railroad brought significant numbers of Irish to Concord. Irish laborers were hired in 1846 to lay the track from Boston through Concord to Fitchburg. Immigrant Irish families lived at first in shanties around Walden Pond. They found opportunities to work as farm laborers. Girls and young women were hired to be servants on large farms and in town. Joining the Hagertys before the Civil War were the McManus, Algeo, Flannery, Loftus, Dempsey, Byron, and Bulger families, and many more who came and moved on in search of other opportunities. In 1863 the Roman Catholic

---

Seated: Timothy and Catherine Goulding. They were early Irish immigrants to Concord and were married in St. Bernard's Church in 1864, a year after Catholics founded the parish. Timothy Goulding was a track hand on the railroad until he bought a farm on Fairhaven Road. Standing: a cousin, Patrick A. Hayes, and their son, John H. Goulding. Circa 1900. (Courtesy of Anna Goulding Manion)

151   The Immigrant Experience

diocese bought the Universalist church building in Monument Square and established St. Bernard's Parish to serve Concord's growing Irish population.

By the 1870s and 1880s, the Irish were sufficiently prosperous to purchase their own farms. They shared in the production of vegetables for the Boston market. According to Edward McCaffrey, his grandfather Michael McCaffrey was the first farmer in Concord to use horses on his farm, replacing oxen, which had been used since the seventeenth century. This change was so popular that other farmers commissioned McCaffrey to buy horses for them in Canada. The animals were sent to Concord by rail.

Jeremiah Sheehan and Terence Magurn, natives of Ireland, owned two of Concord's more flourishing farms. In 1895 the *Concord Enterprise* noted that Sheehan had built a barn, measuring eighty-four by forty feet, on Main Street in West Concord at the site of the Concord Greene. "A barn-warming was held with more than 500 guests who danced til 2:00 A.M." Sheehan came from Ireland in 1858 and had to battle with the New England soil. His grandson, Edward Sheehan, describes him as "a dirt farmer. No, he was a rock farmer. He used to bury rocks!" Magurn was one of the first Concord farmers to use greenhouses. On the eve of World War I, he had a work force of a score of farm laborers harvesting cucumbers, lettuce, and strawberries.

Concord's Irish moved into other professions too. Frank McManus acquired a

livery stable, Maurice McWalter set up a shoe store, and Joseph Dee became an undertaker with Willard Farrar. Concord's entire police force—William Craig and Patrick Varley—was Irish. "We were really scared of them," Louis Venti recalls, "because if we ever got out of line, they wouldn't hesitate to give you a good boot and then tell your father. You got double when you got home! But they were very nice people, and we really respected them a lot."

The Irish lived all over Concord, and their farms circled the town. From the 1870s to the 1920s, there was a heavy concentration of Irish "back of the depot." At that time, three-quarters of the families in that area and along Cottage Lane were of Irish background.

By 1900 Irish girls and boys attended college. The Reverend Matthew Flaherty, pastor of St. Bernard's during the subsequent decade, supported and encouraged families that had aspirations for their children. Concord's Irish women entered the teaching profession in large numbers. Concordians recall Emma Clahane, Helen Nagle, and Margaret Connell, beginning teachers who were hired in Concord at an annual salary of $200 in 1901.

The Knights of Columbus, founded in 1890, and the Ancient Order of Hibernians became important social outlets for Irish men. The Knights of Columbus gave yearly minstrel shows in the 1920s and 1930s. In the early years, membership in the Knights as well as the Hibernians was exclusively Irish.

In 1887 Concord's Irish mounted a successful campaign for political office. At stake was a seat on the school committee. The Irish, who comprised about one-third of the total population and a greater portion of the school population because of their high birth rate, felt disenfranchised and threatened by Protestant dominance in the public schools. The Reverend John A. Crowe, assistant pastor of St. Bernard's, agreed to run for school committee and won. Many Yankees were appalled. One of Concord's more prominent citizens noted in his diary on 25 March 1887, "The caucus—a mob of Irish nominating the Priest for school committee and squelching Thompson." At first, Crowe had a difficult time influencing the school committee, but the precedent, once established, was never to be challenged. Daniel McSweeny, Thomas Shaughnessy, and Thomas Powers each took his place on the school committee. In 1914 Father Flaherty was elected chairman.

Irish have traditionally gravitated toward politics in America. In Concord they served on many town boards and, in 1922, won their first selectman's race. Irish in Concord, as elsewhere in the nation, found a home in the Democratic party. After World War I, and well past World War II, Concord's Irish held the majority of seats on the town's Democratic Committee. Canadians, Norwegians, and Italians tended, on the other hand, to join the Republican party when they became citizens and exercised their political rights.

Bigotry was not, of course, confined to

The Reverend John A. Crowe, assistant pastor of St. Bernard's Church. Circa 1900. (Courtesy of St. Bridget's Church, Maynard)

Concord. The American Protective Association was formed in 1894 to combat the rising influence of immigrant groups, especially those that were predominantly Catholic. That same year, the APA decided to hold a convention in Concord's Town House. The APA had support in Concord, as several residents were actively involved in the state organization, but when the APA delegates arrived by train in Concord, they were greeted with a demonstration. Bricks and stones, as well as epithets, were hurled, and the delegates soon scrambled back onto the train at the

Lowell Road depot. Terry McHugh recalls his parents and older brothers telling the tale. "The Irish had many Yankee friends who were right there with them, chasing the APA back to Boston."

Concord's Irish (and Italians) suffered from class distinctions and religious prejudice more than other ethnic groups. The gulf was noticeable on Sunday mornings when groups walked to church at St. Bernard's and the First Parish. Catholics sensed that Protestants felt they had the edge in status. The distinction was carried to extremes with the recognition among many Concordians that Snow's Pharmacy was the "Catholic" drugstore and Richardson's was "Protestant." One Irish-Catholic woman recalls her father's admonishing her for frequenting Richardson's by saying: "Don't you know you should trade with your own kind?" A story told countless times, always with great laughter, concerned a woman named Murphy who lived on Nashawtuc Hill in the 1920s. The Murphys were Canadian and Protestant. To distinguish themselves from the Irish, she always referred to herself as "Mrs. Murfay."

The Irish had their champions among the Yankees along the way. Ellen Emerson, daughter of Ralph Waldo and Lidian, was instrumental, as a member of the school committee, in hiring the first Irish Catholic teachers in Concord. Emma Clahane was a protégée of Ellen Emerson according to Gladys Clark. As time went on,

Concordians of Irish extraction received support from many Yankees in seeking political office. After World War I, mixed marriages were increasingly common.

The Irish experience was not unlike that of the other ethnic groups who found that the neighborhood comraderie was what mattered most. Here, whether it was in back of the depot, Concord Junction, or the East Quarter, they felt no ethnic nor religious prejudice. Neighbors were always there when needed most, and the Irish were eager to provide when others needed them.

The Canadians

Canadians began coming to Concord as early as the 1840s and were second only to the Irish in numbers immigrating to Concord. In 1910 some 400 Concordians listed Canada as their place of birth; 475 listed Ireland.

The first Canadian immigrants were mainly from Nova Scotia, which continued to provide most of the immigrants from Canada into the twentieth century. Louis Surette, father of the composer and musician, Thomas Whitney Surette, was one of

Wedding pictures of Terence McHugh and Mary Dee. They were natives of Ireland and moved to their farm on Lexington Road on St. Patrick's Day, 1880. (Courtesy of Terry McHugh)

the first Nova Scotians to arrive. By 1900 numerous individuals and families were also coming from Quebec, New Brunswick, Prince Edward Island, and Newfoundland.

The serious and lengthy economic decline that began in Nova Scotia in 1867, the year of the Canadian Confederation, explains the great immigration from that province. A massive migration to the United States continued unabated for fifty years and peaked again after World War II. Nova Scotian historian Terence Punch says that the exodus was so large, "it seemed that every Nova Scotian family had a son or daughter in the 'Boston states,' as surplus labor migrated outwards in search of work."

Nova Scotian immigrants to Concord came from all eighteen of the province's counties. Unlike their Norwegian and Italian counterparts, the Nova Scotians did not share a birthplace, and many of them did not have contacts here when they arrived.

Nova Scotia was originally settled by the French, known as Acadians (of Evangeline lore), but large migrations of English and Scottish took place following France's defeat in the colonial wars. Two large migrations of New Englanders to Nova Scotia occurred late in the eighteenth century and included Loyalists who opposed American independence. Many American blacks came during the War of 1812, and freedmen came after the Civil War. Irish arrived in Nova Scotia at the time of the potato famine. The Concordians who came from Nova Scotia mirrored population patterns of their homeland. Their ancestors were French, Scottish, English, both white and black Americans, and Irish.

During the 1870s and 1880s Nova Scotians either replaced or took positions similar to the Irish. Males were largely farm laborers; females were domestics. By the 1880s and 1890s, West Concord's mills were thriving. The population of Concord had begun to expand. There were many opportunities for immigrants. Large numbers of Nova Scotians continued to arrive, joined by immigrants from the other Maritime Provinces.

At the same time, there was a pattern of upward mobility. During the first decade of the twentieth century, as Isaac Beharrell's contracting business expanded, he was able to hire a dozen carpenters and masons, many of them from Canada. Richard and Al Wilson, brothers from Nova Scotia, founded Wilson Lumber Yard. Edward Comeau also went into contracting, a business which was not limited to house building. According to Edward's son Charles, "he'd plow your garden for you, he'd haul the ashes away from your cellar, and dig your foundation for a new home or barn." Many of Comeau's employees were young men from Nova Scotia.

Immigrants from the Maritime Provinces were soon joined by families from Quebec. In 1890 Auguste Moreau and his family came to Concord Center, where he established a blacksmith shop near the depot on Sudbury Road. Charles and Adeline Pageau arrived soon after from Quebec City via Lowell. The Pageaus lived on Cottage Street in West Concord with their five sons and three daughters and Adeline's parents. Charles, three of his sons, and a grandson were carpenters with Isaac Beharrell's firm. Florida Pageau and Leon Christian, grandchildren of Charles, recalled living in the old Concord Junction Depot for two months before their house on Cottage Street was available. The depot had been sold and moved to Derby Street on blocks, advertised as a place to live. "One room included two ticket windows! The building didn't settle properly on the blocks and stood, instead, at an angle. You could sit in the rocking chair in the sitting room, and before you knew it, you were at the other end of the room!"

The harness factory on Main Street employed many Canadians. Harness fitters required a special skill that may have been learned in Canada as most of them were from New Brunswick or Quebec. When the factory closed its doors, many were forced to leave in search of jobs.

Most Canadian immigrants lived in West Concord on Main, Derby, Pine, Central, Highland, and neighboring streets. They participated in the founding of Our Lady Help of Christians and the West Concord Union churches. They did not organize their own social clubs or char-ities but quickly joined those already in existence.

The French-Canadians from Quebec usually spoke French in their homes. Their children learned English in the Concord schools but were expected to converse with their parents in French. The small number of Quebecois made it difficult to retain their heritage. Most attended Our Lady's parish, but the church was largely Irish and left little opportunity to honor saints or observe holidays from the French Canadian tradition. Like all immigrant groups in Concord, however, the French Canadians continued to sing familiar tunes and prepare familiar foods, which in their case included pea soup and French raisin and salmon pies.

The Norwegians

Norwegians came to Concord at a time when large numbers of Scandinavians emigrated to America. Most chose the Midwest and the prairie as their destination, but some chose Massachusetts as their new home.

In the late nineteenth and early twentieth centuries, it was difficult to make more than a subsistence living in Norway. Lars Anderson, who came to Concord from Loiten in 1889, wrote about his youth in Norway on a small farm.

"The crops are very uncertin it is either too much rain and the soil not deep enough

on the top of the ledge and then every thing turns pale. If the season is dry it all dries up. Once in a great while it will be just a little rain and a little sunshine and then one can get a crop, which consist of Potatoes, Oats, Rye and Barley. That is something to live on during the year but nothing that anyone can get any cash out of. I was seventeen years old when my poor Father died. We was not able to run the Farm any longer and we Failed. Everything was sold to benefit the creditors . . . I tried my best to get a job whereby i could suport my mother and myself. I was turned down everyplace, nobody wonted me. In the first plase i only had a simple education. Another thing that stood in my way was that i was poor. That is a great handicap over there. That is one reason whi i like the U.S. A poor boy if he is honest and up right, hi can make good much easier than in Norway. My good sister had been over here about four years and she came to my resque she sent us a letter and ticket for both my Mother and i and that is how i came to the U.S.A. and thanks be to God that i came here. It was the best thing for The Lord has Blessed me Greatly." Lars Anderson's market, which he bought

---

Isaac Beharrell, elevated, in white shirt and bowler hat, on the steps of his contracting firm. Front row, second and third from left, George and Aimee Pageau; second row, left, Leon Pageau; second from right, Charles Pageau. Circa 1905. (Courtesy of Leon Christian)

from Mr. Towle and Mr. Kent, was until recently a Main Street landmark.

There were many opportunities in Concord for Norwegians. Single men worked as farm laborers, and young women worked as cooks and maids. Few came with their families. Passage was often paid by the prospective employer, in exchange for the promise of a year's work. One Concord farmer hired Norwegians to work for a year without salary, providing only room and board, tobacco, and lessons in reading and writing English.

Despite the hardships, life in Concord offered possibilities of success and happiness enough to attract many siblings in Norway. Beckvolds, Thorpes, Petersens, Helshers, Olsens, Hansens, Nelsons, Engebretsens, and Andersens arrived in Concord between the 1880s and World War I, many of them from Loiten. (Waco, Texas, was the other place to which people from Loiten emigrated in large numbers!) Since Scandinavians often took their fathers' first names as their own last names, many Andersens, Olsens, and Petersens were not related. Concord's Norwegian community was soon large enough to establish families. At first, most married spouses from their homeland, although a number married Swedes and Danes. Close associations with fellow Scandinavians developed.

The Scandinavian Temperance Society, organized in 1885, met monthly in the vestry of the Trinitarian Congregational Church. Its officers included Ole Thorpe, president, who also served as minister to

160   The Immigrant Experience

Norwegians who used the church for their services, his brother Emil, vice president, and Lars Anderson, recording secretary. The Norwegian and Danish Methodist Episcopal Church was organized in 1887, and a church was built at the corner of Thoreau Street and Thoreau Court six years later. In 1894 another congregation of Norwegians formed the Evangelical Free Church, holding services in the Trinitarian Congregational Church. Herbert Peterson, whose father came from Stockholm and whose mother was born to Danish immigrants, recalls attending Sunday morning services at the Thoreau Street church. He couldn't understand a word of the sermon, which was in Norwegian, but each week after the service he enjoyed talking with the Scandinavian girls who were domestics on Main Street, Nashawtuc Hill, and Monument Street. It was well worth the time; Peterson met his future wife after one of these services.

Norwegians founded other local associations. The Sons of Norway, a fraternal organization, thrived in the decades after 1910. It engaged in promoting friendship, charity, and athletic events. Norwegian prowess in tugs of war was legendary. The Sick Benefit Society, active in the 1920s and 1930s, raised money for the elderly.

Norwegian men did not remain farm laborers for long. Several of the men, includ-

Birthplace of Lars Anderson in Loiten, Norway. Circa 1890. (Courtesy of William Anderson)

Left to right: Karl, Emil, Krist, Julia, and Margit Andersen. Krist Andersen: "I was born across the waters in a little town in Norway called Loiten. The picture was taken in 1914, the day we left for America." (Courtesy of Krist Andersen)

ing Christian Benson, Martinus Helsher, and Lars and Rudolf Petersen, became owners of large farms on Barrett's Mill Road, Westford Road, and Monument Street. Others became carpenters or

In formidable pose, the Sons of Norway's tug of war team are, left to right: Henry Bertelsen, Mathias Andreasen, Gustav Jensen, Ole Burstad, Hans Nashe, Herman Hansen. Circa 1915. (Courtesy of Edith Hansen Christiansen)

Martinus Helsher leaving his farm on Westford
Road with a load of vegetables for the Boston
market. Circa 1900. (Courtesy of Harriet
Helsher)

worked in the mills. Edwin Edwardsen, as a boy, worked a sixty-hour week at the looms in the Strathmore Woolen Mill before World War I for which he was paid $5.22.

Class distinctions were clearly drawn. In school the children of well-to-do families didn't mingle with the children of Norwegian immigrants. Young Norwegian women who worked as nursemaids or cooks were expected to eat in the kitchen. Many old Norwegian families recall their mothers or aunts working as maids, cooks, and nurses for young children. As servants, they would often overhear the gossip about town politics that would take place when Concord families entertained. They delighted in passing on this information and in anticipating a turn in political events that others read with surprise when announced in the local newspaper.

Norwegians who were not engaged in farming lived in the center of town. Some lived back of the depot among large numbers of Irish and several Italian families. Others lived with Irish, Italians, and Jews behind St. Bernard's Church on Bedford Court and Davis Court. A few lived in Concord Junction. In general, assimilation came easily to the Norwegians. Their Protestant faith was, undoubtedly, a significant factor in this regard. Little effort was made to retain their language. They appeared to win acceptance readily, and whatever discrimination they experienced was social rather than ethnic.

The Italians

Alessandro and Maria Macone, Salvatore and Clorinda Bartolomeo and Salvatore's brother John, and Salvatore and Benedetta Palmaccio came from Gaeta and the neighboring town of Formia, not far from Naples, in the 1890s, to settle in Concord. The Macones bought a farm on Strawberry Hill Road. The Bartolomeos established a fruit store on Commonwealth Avenue, and John Bartolomeo and Salvatore Palmaccio drove a horse and wagon throughout neighboring towns, selling the fruit from house to house. Before long John Bartolomeo had his own store on Thoreau Street in Concord Center.

Italy as a nation faced immense economic problems in the 1890s and early 1900s. Thousands of Italian men came to the United States to provide money for their families at home. Some hoped to establish themselves in America and were thus willing to go wherever the work was. In August 1892 the *Concord Enterprise* reported that "a large gang of Italians recently appeared in town, employed at the Nashawtuc Farm." In 1898 Concord decided to build a sewer system. The Boston contractor who won the bid arrived with two hundred Italian laborers who lived in shanties in the field by the Sudbury River between Lowell Road and Egg Rock. The situation was similar to the building of the Fitchburg Railroad in the 1840s by the

Alessandro and Maria Macone host a Sunday afternoon gathering at their Strawberry Hill farm. Alessandro is on the left, standing in profile; Maria is standing in the center wearing a black blouse. Circa 1905. (Courtesy of Peanut Macone)

Irish who lived in shanties near Walden Pond.

Among the laborers engaged in the sewer construction were Bernardo Venti and his son Guiseppi. Guiseppi's son, Louis Venti, says, "My grandfather brought my father with him from Italy when he was ten years old. He served as the errand boy and did the cooking for the Italian men. They weren't too welcome because they were foreigners. They had to stay by themselves because they didn't know the language to get along with other people."

The pattern of Italian migration did not vary. "When my father came over here," Joseph Bartolomeo says, "it was twenty-five dollars from Naples to New York in steerage. He slept on the floor." Fathers came first, worked to establish themselves, and often worked almost as hard to persuade their spouses to leave their homeland. Jenny DeSalvatore recalls her mother, Josephine Mancuso, flatly refusing the entreaties of her husband to join him in Concord. Only the shock of the devastating 1908 earthquake that destroyed their home in Sicily made her change her mind.

Large numbers of Italians came to Concord between 1910 and 1930. Increasingly, they came from Sicily rather than the

mainland. Eventually, half of Concord's Italians were Sicilians, and the majority of them came from Faro Superiore and adjoining towns. Domenica Scimone describes her expectations when she, her mother, and siblings left Faro Superiore to join her father in Concord. "We were supposed to land in New York but instead landed in Rhode Island and came by train and bus to Concord. In Italy everyone was told the streets were paved with gold. When I arrived in Concord at age six, I bent down to touch the ground, and it was just plain dirt."

Dialect and tradition tended to separate the Sicilians from other Italian immigrants. The Sicilians lived on Bedford and Davis courts and bought farms on Bedford Street. Italians from villages near Rome and Naples and in the Abruzzi lived in back of the depot. There was a mixture in West Concord, where a number of Italian families lived on Conant and Damon streets. An apartment building, off Old-Stow Road, known as the Hill Block, housed Italians from 1914 until the 1930s. "The six families in that building were all Italians," Pasquale Melisi remembers. "Muscato, Ruggerio, Moscariello, Spinelli were some of the families. We were crowded in the apartments. None of us could speak English, but we picked up a few words in East Boston where we first lived." As a boy, Melisi could not always understand his own Italian neighbors because they came from different parts of Italy and spoke different dialects.

Salvatore Bartolomeo driving his fruit cart in a Fourth of July parade at the Concord Junction. Circa 1915. (Courtesy of Bill Shaughnessy)

Birthplace in Faro Superiore, Sicily, of Angelo,
Dominic, and Santo Inferrera. Their parents
and sister perished in the house pictured above
in the 1908 earthquake. The brothers immi-
grated to Concord after World War I. (Photo by
Dominic Inferrera, Jr. Circa 1955.)

The Italians in the Hill Block worked in the mills in West Concord and Maynard and on the railroad. Other Italians worked as gardeners for estates or as masons. The Ventis, DiCiccos, and others worked for the town at the Board of Public Works and other municipal departments. Italian women usually remained at home, raising their families. Unlike the women from Norway, Ireland, and Canada, single Italian women did not come alone to Concord. Such independence was not acceptable. Italians, in particular those from Sicily, worked as farm laborers, rented land, and eventually bought their own farms. Most of the farms in Concord are owned by Scimones, Palumbos, Rotondos, Amendolias, Inferreras, Arenas, and other first- and second-generation Concordians from Faro Superiore.

In Faro Superiore, farm families would go to the highest point around to winnow their wheat, Frank Scimone remembers. "They would wait until a wind came up and throw the wheat up into the air, allowing the chaff to blow away with the wind and the grain to fall to the ground beneath them." Frank's father, also Frank, used the same technique with shell beans on their Bedford Street farm. "On a windy day following the harvest, he would mount a large step ladder, carrying a bushel of the beans. Heaving the basket, he would throw the beans into the air. The beans would fall onto a canvas below, and the lighter scraps of vines and pods would blow off with the wind." Working without

the plateau in Faro was a bit of a hardship!

Like other immigrants, Italians tried to preserve their identity. Italian was usually spoken at home, so the children grew up bilingual. In 1934 Concord organized a chapter of the Sons of Italy, which included daughters as well. According to Carmela Lombardo, a founder and treasurer, the club, led by her uncle Charles Lombardo, sponsored fairs and dances, helped newly arrived Italian immigrants, and worked to preserve the Italian heritage.

At the same time, Italians strove for assimilation and acceptance. Many of them anglicized their names, especially their given names. Guiseppi became Joseph and Giovanna, Jenny. By World War II, intermarriage between Italians and others was common. Though numerous, they never equaled the Irish in number and were thus perceived as less threatening by the native-born population that included almost as many Irish as Yankees. Still, certain incidents spoke to existing prejudice. John Bartolomeo's first job in Concord was as a farm laborer on Virginia Road. According to his son Joseph, "When he and other Italian immigrants went into town on Saturday night, they would get stones and rocks thrown at them. They would be told to go back where they came from. My father couldn't understand how in a country like America that could happen. On that farm they slept in a barn—no house." It was not long, however, before John Bartolomeo

The Concord chapter of the Sons of Italy receiving its charter in August 1934. Concord members are interspersed with unidentified Maynard and Marlboro members. First row, second from left: Santo Inferrara, fifth from left: Peter DeSalvatore, seventh from left:

Nicolo Zaino, Alfred Dentino, Carmela Lombardo, Angelina Girardi, Pasquale Melisi, Velina Bregoli, Jennie Viscariello, Mary Bregoli, Augustine Soffriti, Alipio Pucci, Charles Lombardo, Salvatore Nocella. Second

row: behind A. Girardi: Jennie Scarpetti, Giacomo Rizzitano, Enrichetta Viola, Antonio Amendolia; behind V. Bregoli: Mary Di Meo; behind A. Soffriti: Tito Florio. Fourth row behind N. Zaino: John Marabello; in doorway wearing glasses: Guiseppi Rizzitano. Back row, second from left: Joseph Lombardo, Silvio Trabucco, Anthony Giusti, Daniel Faieta. Third from right, in back: Antonino Amendolia. (Courtesy of Carmela Lombardo)

had his own market on Thoreau Street, the steps of which served as a meeting place for neighborhood kids in the early evening.

Mike Lombardo, whose parents came from the Italian village of Trippi, notes as he looks back on growing up in the town he has served, "I like to think we got a better education here in Concord than the students in the surrounding towns of my era. We sat beside the rich Wasps—we knew who they were, and they knew who we were. It wasn't until World War II that suddenly we were all equal for who we were as people, and not where we were on the economic scale or what ethnic group we might have come from."

Other Immigrants

Most, but not all, of Concord's immigrants came from Ireland, Canada, Norway, and Italy. A large number of young women came from Finland to work in Concord as domestics in the early part of the twentieth century and eventually settled in Maynard. Many Poles came to work as farm laborers at the same time, but they too did not remain in Concord.

In 1901 Concord's first Jews arrived, Samuel and Celia Jacobs, from Vilna, Lithuania. He had a tailor shop on Main Street, which at his death was sold to Max Arkin, a Russian immigrant. Other Jewish families followed in the teens and twenties. The men worked as tailors, ran dry goods establishments, or found jobs in

the mills in West Concord. Each family, Silverman, Fritz, London, found assimilation relatively easy in Concord. Sam Arkin joined his brother Max in Concord in the thirties. He provides a clue to understanding the process of acceptance when he remembers, "Like everyone else, I registered Republican in Concord, but in my head and in my heart, I was always a Democrat." Children of Jewish immigrants, without exception, cherish the memory of growing up in Concord. The numbers, until recently, were always small and never perceived as threatening. And three Jewish families, who came to Concord long after the Jacobs and Arkins, thought they were the town's first Jews.

Norwegians were joined in Concord by Swedes and Danes. Many Swedes worked as laborers and servants for established families. Carl Hay, who came from Sweden in 1900, opened a shoe store. The sons of Peter and Anna Petersen, who came from Denmark in 1875, ran the Concord Clothing Store, which, like the Hay Shoe store, is still in the family.

Immigrants came from other countries in smaller numbers. Maude and Minna Findeisen, dedicated Concord school teachers, were daughters of German immigrants. Matthew Steinmann, foreman at the harness factory, came from Switzerland. Ivan Servais, from Belgium, was a manager at the Strathmore Woolen Mill and became a Concord selectman. Joseph Kulcsar, from Hungary, and Frank Almada, from Portugal, had barbershops in

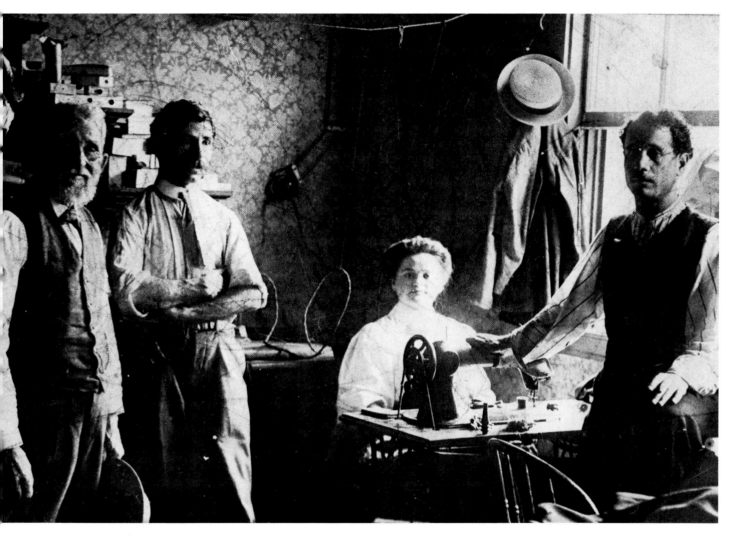

Samuel Jacobs's tailor shop on Main Street
above Vanderhoof's Hardware, circa 1907. Jacobs is second from the left with unidentified
employees. (Courtesy of Ida Jacobs Israel)

town. Sing Wah and Chong Wong, from China, ran laundries in downtown Concord and in Concord Junction.

Concord's black population dwindled as the nineteenth century drew to a close. The Dugan, Garrison, and Robbins families died out. The 1910 census lists six black Concordians, all single adults. The number of blacks began to grow after World War II, but not until 1970 did it equal the number recorded in the mid-nineteenth century. Even then, the figure represented a much smaller percentage of the total population than it had a century earlier.

* * *

The Ancient Order of Royal Hibernians, the Sons of Norway, and the Sons of Italy are gone. Marriages and politics cross ethnic and religious lines. Ethnicity no longer delineates neighborhoods. Still, memory and heritage live on. Ethnicity continues to strengthen individual bonds, but living together has created ties that transcend national origins.

Herbert Peterson who is Scandinavian and Protestant recalls suffering an appendicitis attack in 1911, when he was sixteen, after a long day of working on his parents' farm on Old Bedford Road. He was carried half conscious to his bed. "When I awoke, there was old Mr. McHugh, an Irish Catholic, on his knees next to my bed, praying for me." This was no surprise. Peterson's family shared a common bond

with the Irish farmers in the neighborhood—Magurns, McHughs, Daltons, and Burkes, as well as other Scandinavians and Yankees—Carlsons and Clarks. "If a storm came up suddenly and your hay was still out, neighbors would appear and offer a hand."

Louis Venti speaks for many Concordians who recall their youth in this town: "I think it was because the atmosphere between the various ethnic groups created really one group. You had the Norwegians, Italians, Canadians, Irish, and we all seemed to get along, especially in this area around the depot where I have always lived. I think it was because we were all the same class. I will have to say there were some people who didn't want to associate with the lower classes. But all of us here got along as one and helped each other. My best friend was a Yankee."

Works Consulted

Anderson, Lars. [A Brief Memoir, n.d.].
Concord List of Taxpayers, 1890-1980.
Concord Town Directories, 1892-1937.
Concord Town Reports, 1845-1980.
Concord Vital Statistics: Births, Marriages and Deaths.
Loiten Historical Society, *Lautin Year Book, 1968*, Loiten, Norway.
Punch, Terrence M. "Researching Nova Scotian Ancestry," *New England Historical and Genealogical Register,* Oct., 1984.
Taped interviews with Concordians.
United States Census, Concord, 1840, 1850, 1860, 1880, 1900, 1910.

18
Celebrations

1925, A Nation Is 150

Concord has always treated the Nineteenth of April with a special reverence. The pitch of excitement and the fervor of the preparations become even more intense when Patriots Day and a special milestone of the nation's birthday is reached.

In 1925 the town had geared itself to expect vast crowds, but mother nature had other plans and left a covering of snow and bitter cold temperatures for the big parade. "They waited twenty-five years for it and they couldn't have had a worse day— the snow and the cold," recalls Joseph Dee, who manned the armory headquarters for the parade. Terry McHugh describes the sight of Tom Finan, who served on the police force for many years, "dressed just like the Minuteman with shirt sleeves rolled up. He held that pose throughout the parade and later went to the hospital with pneumonia as a result." Peanut Macone remembers "the tremendous fireworks" and the reenactment of the battle at the North Bridge. "In the sham battle, they were all shivering. Those that had to drop in the snow, I felt sorry for."

Charlie Comeau's father was in charge of supporting the North Bridge from underneath. "They were afraid that the marching feet would cause the bridge to collapse," says Comeau. "We had to truck in extra chairs for the armory for United States Vice President Charles Dawes and get them out again for the dance. I can still see Elsie Rose, the town clerk, and a handsome woman, riding on a float with her cheeks turning blue." Many an enterprising entrepreneur was hurt that day including the young Comeau's aunt and uncle. "My aunt and uncle paid considerably for the privilege of having a concession stand on Lexington Road. My aunt had a caterer make up cakes and sandwiches, and because of the bitter cold about all they sold was coffee, and my friend and I cleared about two acres on Everett Street for parking spaces and the only automobiles we had parked were our own."

Roger Fenn viewed the parade perched on top of his fallen horse's head, trying to keep the horse calm. The day's unexpected turn of events would continue at the festivities held at the armory. Though he didn't have a ticket for admission, he accompanied a relative in and found himself seated at the table with the guests of honor, occupying the vacant place set aside for General John J. Pershing!

Concord at 300

When Concord celebrated its 300th birthday, Franklin Roosevelt, who most Concor-

176 Celebrations

dians did not help elect, was in the White House, and townspeople were coping with the most severe economic depression this country had experienced.

Prices reflected the times. A pound bag of coffee could be purchased for fifteen cents, four pounds of bananas for twenty-one cents, and Anderson's grocery on Main Street was selling swordfish for thirty-two cents a pound. Sound had been introduced to movies, which cost as little as ten to twenty cents. Playing in Concord area theaters at the time were Warner Oland and Stepin Fetchit in *Charlie Chan in Egypt,* Loretta Young and Charles Boyer in *Shanghai,* James Cagney and Pat O'Brien in *The Irish in Us,* Noel Coward in *The Scoundrel,* and Shirley Temple in *Curly Top.*

The busy months of preparation focused on four days of events, from September 11 through September 14, under the direction of Tercentenary Chairman, H. Whittemore Brown. Invited dignitaries, such as Governor James Michael Curley, and descendants of longtime Concord families living out of state, gathered with local townspeople to share in the celebration. The events received wide coverage in the Boston papers, while at home the founding editor of the *Concord Journal,* Wentworth Stewart, called for a transfusion of the Concord spirit to a world threatened by dictatorship.

Marching down the Milldam in the 1925 parade. (Courtesy of the Concord Free Public Library)

The sun shone on the majestic parade, led by Chief Marshall Michael Dee, as crowds lined the streets and groups gathered on nearby lawns. Seventy-four imaginative floats representing community organizations and businesses were displayed. Among the prize winning floats were those of the West Concord Village Improvement Society showing three centuries of progress; the Reformatory School, designed and built by the inmates displaying the skills learned at the prison trade school; the New Mode Beauty Shoppe with Elsie Rose, as a hoop-skirted belle standing over an auto from Middlesex Motors; and local youth riding old-fashioned large wheeled bicycles presented by Macone's Sporting Goods store. Local sporting events drew many viewers. The largest gathering was at the Saturday baseball game between the Concord Tercentenarians and the Lincoln Mohawks, held on the Emerson Playground, with Concord victorious by a score of five to three.

A high point of the celebration was *The Drama of Concord*. A cast of 245 took part in the pageant staged at the Veterans Building and written by Allen French. Through two readers, one representing the Spirit of History and the other the Spirit of Concord, the story of the town was told from the days of the purchase of land from the Indians to the Civil War. Actors portrayed the scenes on stage as a series of living pictures.

Over 500 persons attended the Tercentenary Ball held at the Armory, with 180 couples entering the grand march, many

Elsie Rose is the belle enveloping the car, as
the New Mode Beauty Shoppe float rides by in
the 1935 parade. (Courtesy of the Concord Free
Public Library)

Macone Brothers Sporting Goods float. Left to
right: Patty Hosmer, Bill Harlow, William
Wadsworth, Helen Wadsworth, Peanut
Macone, Ginny Biggi, Whitney Smith, Betty
Brooks, Jack Edmonds, Clara Wadsworth.
1935. (Collection of the Concord Historical
Commission, courtesy of Peanut Macone)

in costumes. Jazz was king then and Cab Calloway's orchestra from New York City's Cotton Club was the evening's dance band as well as entertainment. The choice of Calloway drew surprised comment by certain of the Boston papers. "The African tempo and howls of hi-de-ho-de-ho" was seen by some reporters as an odd choice for descendants of the Minuteman. The *Concord Journal,* however, commented that "the guests seemed to be enjoying the contortions and eccentricities of Cab Calloway and while the performance put on by his musicians seemed to be a spectacular show rather than the playing of dance tunes, none was disappointed. Their rendition of a Sousa march was in excellent style!"

Also part of the 1935 celebration was the dedication of seventy acres of the Hap-good Wright Town Forest, a far-sighted birthday gift presented to Concord by a resident in 1885 when the town turned 250 years old. Hapgood Wright, born in Concord, was seventy-four years old when he gave the land to the town. When he made the land gift he also presented the town with $1,000 to be held in trust for fifty years. The interest was to be used for some needed purpose and the principal to be held for another fifty years. In 1935 more than $600 had been realized from this fund. Wright, in his will, named two funds of $1,000 to be placed at interest, one until 1985 and the other until 2035, at the end of which time the interest may be spent and the principal to earn interest for another 100 and 150 years, allowing Concord in the year 2035 to spend the interest from all three funds at once.

19

Facing up to the Great Depression

There are events that are watersheds in men's lives and become reference points afterwards in time. Such an event was the stock market crash of 1929, which shattered confidence, altered the scope of and reliance on government, and affected everyone in some manner.

Though in September of 1929 the stock market broke, rallied, and then broke again, it was the violent downward spiraling of stock market prices during the last week in October, precipitating the severe national depression that followed, that has come to be known as the crash of 1929. A local newspaper always plays an important part in the life of a small town and the *Concord Journal,* founded in 1928, played its part in such a time of crisis. Information was disseminated about available jobs and fund-raising events for the unemployed, town policies relating to local relief were explored, and in a time when people stayed close to home, the *Journal* publicized available local entertainment such as the popular minstrel shows, performances by the Concord Players, and movies shown at the armory.

The editorial page of Wentworth Stewart, the *Journal*'s editor and publisher,

rang like sermons from the pulpit. At times he would view the depression as a moral cleansing of the national soul, a chance to work off excesses, and in other instances he was determined to buoy up the flagging spirit and encourage positive thinking. "The crash," he wrote, "came about in large part by an army of gamblers from all walks of life who had sought easy money . . . Adjusting to a new standard of normalcy, our former idea of normal conditions was extravagant, unwarranted. When business practices become wild then business is imperiled." One editorial was titled, "Laughter As A Cure For Depression," and on 1 September 1932 a special confidence issue of the *Journal* was printed promoting local trade, encouraging business confidence, and urging community cooperation. One local correspondent for the *Journal* at this time was Marian Miller. Her father, Clarence H. Blackall, an architect best known for designing the Colonial and Wilbur theatres and the Copley Plaza Hotel, was "wiped out by the crash. People were very anxious during this period and didn't know what was coming next."

Those with jobs often found their pay reduced and Concord town employees and teachers took salary cuts. "I took a slice in pay like a lot of other people," recalls Joe Dee who was custodian at the armory. "Though Concord had a rural flavor to it fifty years ago, a number of its people worked in Boston, in the financial end, and were hurt. For those who were prosperous, it was a longer drop and a bigger thud."

There was an expressed determination by the town fathers that no family would be in need as long as there were resources available. The Board of Selectmen in November 1930 made an appeal "to those planning to have work done on their homes to do it now. Remember every man or woman who can work and earn and buy helps to keep others at work." Those with work to offer and those who needed work were requested to contact the selectmen. Work for the unemployed was found with the water, sewer, and highway departments. Men could be seen cutting brush along Seven Star Lane and Virginia Road and replacing inadequate pipes on Bradford and Maple streets. Women were employed sewing and knitting garments which were distributed among the needy. Many Concord men were also able to obtain work on the construction of the new Concord by-pass, later known as Route 2.

Private groups, such as the Female Charitable Society, which became Concord Family Service, the Oddfellows, and individual churches appealed for funds for the needy. Concord with its abundance of farm produce enlisted in the relief of conditions in Boston. The Trinitarian Congregational Church undertook to act as collector of surplus fruit and vegetables in Concord to be distributed in Boston by the City Mis-

sion Society to families whose wage earners were out of work, and grocer Leslie Anderson volunteered to transport the produce each week.

Archie Ferran worked the evening shift at the *Boston Globe* and never forgot the sight of "all those homeless men setting up camp on the Boston Common and waiting for food to be deposited from restaurants into garbage cans. Concord never experienced the agony of the depression the way I saw it in Boston." Despite individual hardship, there was a determined spirit in the town and a willingness to look out for those in need. "I was married in 1930, and like everyone else felt the pinch," recalls Charlie Comeau. "The depression is an experience I hope we never have to go through again. What was wonderful though was the way we all stuck together." "Life was at a slower pace then, the town was smaller, and you really had neighbors you knew back in those days," adds Joseph Dee.

Mrs. Leslie Moore of the Women's Club chaired "an impromptu university" during the winter of 1933 consisting of seventeen classes, each with a volunteer instructor. "When local funds ran out it never occurred to the selectmen that they could do no more," observes David Little. "If public funds were exhausted, they reasoned, an appeal must be made for private aid. Hayden Whitney initially put up money as a loan to the town to do public works from which the Unemployment Relief Committee consisting of private citizens was

Local ads reflect the needs and reduced purchasing power of an economy in depression. 1932. (Courtesy of the *Concord Journal*)

formed. This was an illustration of what a community could do for itself."

The funds raised by this committee of private citizens were, according to the 1932 Town Report, "of the greatest help in providing for employment during that year." Roger Fenn, who had opened the Fenn School weeks before the crash, strongly defended the unemployed against charges of their unwillingness to work in a letter to the editor of the *Concord Journal* in December 1932: "One hears an unfortunate amount of talk these days to the effect that Concord's unemployed do not want to work, and that when they do work they not only work badly but want higher than standard pay . . . Possibly I have just been lucky, but if others with good reports to make would gossip as freely as those with the bad reports, perhaps we would run less risk of discrediting the whole group of jobless men to the serious hardship of some of our most deserving and innocent fellow citizens."

To provide relief for the jobless, President Herbert Hoover relied on local government initiative and private charity but was firmly against all proposals for federal relief. Concord was a strongly Republican town in those days and voted for Hoover in 1932 despite the national landslide for Franklin Roosevelt. Whether reflecting Concord's political sentiment or influencing it, *Concord Journal* editor Stewart stood firmly in the Hoover camp. "Franklin Roosevelt," he wrote, "has encouraged a vastly extended lunatic fringe, many of

them sincere and earnest, but are in straits that lead them to fall under the spell of this modern Santa Claus."

"Roosevelt," observes Marian Miller, "was not a favorite of my husband, but he had a definite appeal to some in town. Where there was a steady following for Hoover, Roosevelt generated more enthusiasm and had a more excitable following."

Enthusiasm for Roosevelt is expressed by Joseph Dee. "When Roosevelt came in things were rock bottom. He was a breath of life and jacked up morale. When he would come on the radio—you talk about Geritol—he was a ray of hope."

When the New Deal began, Concord cooperated fully with the national code of fair practices and was one of the "100 percent" towns displaying the blue eagle to show compliance. Elizabeth Brennan, secretary to the Board of Selectmen, chaired a committee to secure the pledge of consumers "to buy only from those employers who have taken the increased burden of increasing payrolls to bring back prosperity." In 1933, with the organization of the federal Public Works Administration (PWA), there was an opportunity for the town to present public works projects which, if approved, would receive an outright grant of 30 percent of the direct cost of the project from the federal government and a loan on favorable terms for the other 70 percent. The Hunt Gymnasium is an example of such a PWA project. In 1928 William Hunt had given $25,000 to the town to build a gymnasium, and a federal grant was secured to make up the $60,000 needed for its construction in 1935.

The creation of the Civil Works Administration resulted in the Board of Selectmen starting a local Civil Works Administration with Mr. Chilton Cabot appointed administrator to take care of re-employment, management of projects, and general administration. A National Re-employment Office was opened in town under the supervision of the federal Department of Labor. Work on the Hapgood Wright Town Forest had its humorous side. Harold Chase remembers an incident involving Bebe Hosmer, "who was in charge of the WPA workers and set out to plant black walnut trees in the forest. He left the walnuts in a pile and when he returned the squirrels had gotten to them. But that's the way trees often get planted anyhow."

Looking back, Concord was able to meet the challenge of a national depression through the pride and ability shown in local government and the sense of neighborliness which existed. These were resources the town possessed which could not be measured in financial terms.

The Library Could Grow in Hard Times

"My father always maintained that if a building is well proportioned, you can finish it in any style you like," recalls David Little, whose father was the architect hired to remodel the Concord Free Public Library in 1930.

The Concord Library when it was built in 1871, at the intersection of Main Street and Sudbury Road, was designed in the half-Gothic, half-mansard style that was popular in that era. The original provision for a library within Concord, however, goes back to 1672 when a committee of citizens instructed the selectmen to form a library, "That care be taken of the Books of Marters and other books, that belong to the Towne, that they be kept from abusive usage, and not be lent to persons more than one month at a time."

When Harry B. Little became the architect to deal with the badly cluttered interior, he proposed to alter the exterior to a Georgian Colonial design. "And as is typical of the Concord character," laughs Little, "there was no consensus of opinion about his proposal." The library was in a sound financial position, the result of a fund left by its founder, William Munroe, in 1873 which had grown to almost $80,000. And precisely at this time, when so much else was unaffordable, patronage of the library was high and circulation exceeded 100,000 by 1932.

If Harry Little favored a new exterior design, he also shared the admiration that people had for the special features of the central octagonal room. "Dad thoroughly cleaned out this extraordinarily handsome room to the point where its architectural features could be viewed. The octagonal

In depression days people stayed close to home
and made extensive use of the town's library facilities. The Loring N. Fowler Memorial
Library in West Concord opened in 1930, and
the extensive remodelling and enlargement of
the Concord Free Public Library was completed
in 1934.

Front exterior and central room views of the
Concord Free Public Library in 1930 before remodelling. (Courtesy of the Concord Free Public Library)

proportions of this center room were now accented by the new Georgian Colonial exterior." Changes within the first-floor interior were designed to accommodate adult and children's reading rooms along with rooms for reference and catalogues, while a special feature of the second floor was the addition of an art gallery.

The record shows that great efforts were undertaken to keep circulation flowing through the frozen pipes of the New England cold. The charge-out desk was temporarily located in the entrance hall of the old high school building, located where the parking lot is now, while the children's books were kept in the cloakroom. And librarians became used to crossing the street to retrieve books from the building under construction. In January 1934, the doors of the remodeled library opened for use, an institution of the town whose origins date back further than any other known in America.

Blowing in the Wind—The 1938 Hurricane

For Concord and the surrounding towns, nature's big onslaught of the century remains the 1938 hurricane.

The man put in charge of the clean-up operations was Elmer Joslin, then Superintendent of Roads and Bridges. On September 21, Joslin was unaware that there was a hurricane on the way. "The weather forecasting in those days didn't amount to much. There was no advance information whatever. It had rained for several days before which made the ground soft. The first call I had was that a tree had fallen across Pine Street and just as I hung up from that call, two or three other calls from West Concord came in, and then more and more trees were reported down. At about midnight we finally realized we were having a hurricane."

Fred Tower, a local cooperative observer for the United States Weather Bureau, read the last measure of his wind gauge at 125 miles per hour before it blew off, says Joslin. "We worked all through the night and at about 3:00 A.M., the selectmen called a meeting at the Town Hall of all the town departments. We were all working on our own areas and they felt there should be a single coordinator. After much discussion, I was appointed to coordinate all the departments in the clean-up and we all worked well together."

Men couldn't tell, he says, if the wires they were trying to untangle from trees were live or not and after several serious accidents, all power was shut off. "As I would get the word from the light plant that wires were clear, then we could go to work on the trees and as fast as we could we opened the streets. Many of Concord's beautiful elm trees were destroyed in the hurricane. Some of them were nearly forty-eight inches in diameter and they formed an arch across Main Street."

Over at Nine Acre Corner, Rusty Wheeler was struggling to get through to

The 1938 hurricane unleashes its fury. The Andrew Hepburn house on Barrett's Mill Road.

Middlesex Institution for Savings on Main Street.

The Alcott house on Lexington Road.

his future wife, Marian. It was their second date and he remembers the tough going on the roads. "The leaves were flying so fast it felt like you were hit by a tree. The greenhouses were being blown apart, the roofs would open up, and the big water pipes were broken." Wheeler had a narrow escape when the large elm in front of St. Bernard's Church crashed to the street, barely missing his car. The *Concord Journal* reported the severe losses suffered by orchards, though Ephraim Bull's original grapevine was spared despite a huge elm that fell close to it. At the reformatory the storm brought down over 200 feet of brick wall and a high wire fence with barbed wire over it was quickly constructed.

The large elm in front of the brick home of architect Andrew Hepburn, at the corner of Lowell and Barrett's Mill roads, was uprooted and, according to the *Journal,* "came crashing down on the old colonial dwelling punctuating the roof and second floor wall and dislodging two chimneys." The elm was considered to be the largest in the state, measuring seventeen feet, four inches in circumference. Similarly the huge elm in front of the Middlesex Institution for Savings crashed on the building, "knocking out one of the four large pillars and tearing a gaping hole in the roof."

Chief of Police William Ryan added twelve special officers to the force already on duty, and they assisted people taking refuge in the Concord Library which was kept open as a shelter. Unlike some other communities, there were no reports of looting, says the newspaper, and Company H, Massachusetts National Guard, which stood ready to help, was never called upon. There were residents who made the best of their loss of light and electricity by regaining a sense of the past. The *Journal* reports that the R. J. Rodday Company in West Concord sold twelve dozen lamp chimneys the morning after the hurricane to customers, "most of whom had not smelled a kerosene lamp for twenty to thirty years. Many of the children were delighted with oil lamps, never having seen them before."

The debris, says Joslin, was dumped in an old deep gravel pit at the corner of Sandy Pond Road. "The owner, a contractor, allowed us to dump all the debris there as we couldn't use our own town dump or we would have filled it up in no time. We had 750 stumps all over town that were removed after the debris was picked up and the streets opened. Some of the trees that blew over were leaning against houses, which made the removal of limbs and the tree difficult without damaging the house further." Lacking the tools to clear away the trees, Joslin sought additional equipment from a wholesale supplier in Boston. "I sent a truck to get two dozen, two-man crosscut saws and six dozen axes, in fact I took all they could spare. It would take two men about three-quarters of an hour to cut a tree by hand. Of course now there are chain saws. I couldn't believe my eyes the first time I saw a man use a chain saw to cut a tree. When I think how we struggled in those days."

The annual report for that year says that a special Town Meeting was held on 19 October 1938. Voters made an emergency appropriation of $25,000 for the purpose of repairing the damage to town property and $22,000 to the Municipal Light Board—significant figures for a time when the nation was starting to recover from the depression, but behind the statistics lay the drama of a community pulling together.

20
We Came On Over

The first Memorial Day parade that Joseph Dee marched in was in 1915. World War I had begun in Europe and the previous December, Dee had joined Company I, registering at the old armory, now 51 Walden. His company was called overseas in 1917 when America entered the war, and during the next two years Dee was in France. It was in 1920 that he was home for good, and for fifty-five years he proudly carried the United States colors for Concord at the head of each parade.

To the memory of Nancy, France, where he was first stationed and "which meant so much to me," Dee named Nancy Road, when he sold land for development in 1954. Close by on Bedford Street stands the family home of the Dees. His service in France also reveals the beautiful story of a friendship forged in wartime. It was the practice of the U.S. Army to make arrangements with French families who would provide shelter for a certain number of soldiers. During the winter of 1918, Dee stayed in the hayloft of a family in the town of Rouceux in the eastern part of France near Alsace Lorraine.

He remembers the warmth of the mother of the family with great affection. "She was like a mother to me. There was many an evening I spent in the family kitchen. I learned considerable French and she asked questions about this country." They both agreed to correspond, and before the war ended, Dee received a letter asking him if he wished to be godfather to the new baby of the family. "I was able to get a pass to visit them the following year. The family had the baptism and I signed the baptismal certificate."

When World War II began, Dee and the family lost contact until one day a letter arrived in Concord from the godchild explaining that her mother had died during the war from lack of medical treatment and asking Dee to continue the correspondence with her. He did and expressed the hope of returning to France one day. In 1967 arrangements were made for him to meet his godchild in the hotel lobby of the town where she was born. "It was quite a moment for me. I had only seen her once, the day she was baptized." His hair had long since turned white and the child, Suzanne, was a woman of forty-nine. Dee remembers with emotion that moment when she walked up to him to ask, "Are you Joseph?" They continued to correspond and while the peace following the war did not last, the relationships formed during the war would endure.

A Tribute to the Doughboy

They lost their lives to "the war to end all wars" and Concord wanted to remember the twenty-five soldiers from their town

Joe Dee on left marches with Arthur Trepanier and Judge David Williams. 1975. (Courtesy of the Joe Dee family)

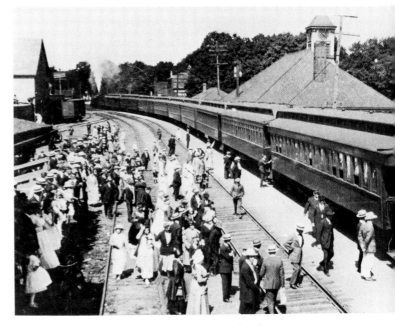

Troop trains leaving for World War I at the depot. (Courtesy of the Concord Free Public Library)

who had fallen. Town Meeting in 1923 authorized the placement of a boulder "as a permanent memorial to those who gave up their lives in the Great War."

A boulder at the farm of Charles and Walter Nelson of Mill Street in Lincoln was selected and the Concord town fathers noted in their annual report "that it was in that part of Lincoln which was formerly Concord." The boulder measured twelve feet by fifteen feet, weighed more than forty tons, and was not easy to move to Monument Square. The Woburn firm of

Moving the World War I Memorial Boulder from Lincoln along Lexington Road to Monument Square. 1924. (Courtesy of the Concord Free Public Library)

Martin Ellis & Co. agreed to the task, supplying the labor with the town providing the hauling equipment. Permission to move the boulder was obtained from the local Department of Public Works headed by Elmer Joslin, who was also a World War I veteran. The boulder was jacked up and loaded onto timbers. The first attempt to hitch up the tractor and roller for a straight pull was found to be impractical because of the lack of traction.

After several attempts, the method that finally proved successful is described by chairman of the Memorial Committee, Judge Prescott Keyes: "A rope was made fast at one end to the steam roller, which was rigged so as to act as a 'dead man.' The rope then passed three times between a pulley block fastened to the boulder and another pulley block fastened to the roller. The tractor would pull until the blocks came close together, when the roller would pull them apart and move forward to a new station." Each pull took about fifteen minutes and carried the boulder forward about fifty feet, and planks had to be laid to protect the surface of the highway from the rollers. Fortunately, the weather was favorable and after twenty-four days the boulder was put in place on December 18.

A highlight of the Memorial Day exercises for 1924 was the dedication of the World War Memorial Boulder before a large gathering of the townspeople. Representatives of the British Naval and Military Veterans Association were present to join in the dedication ceremonies. Taps was sounded in tribute to the dead whose names were inscribed on the boulder along with the words of Emerson:

> So nigh is grandeur to our dust
> So near is god to man
> When duty whispers low thou must
> The youth replies I can.

The Morning of Pearl Harbor

The attack on Pearl Harbor was a cataclysmic event that instantly shattered our nation's neutrality laws, ended the debate

Dalgo Bregoli at Pearl Harbor. (Courtesy of Dalgo Bregoli)

over isolationism, and thrust the United States into the role of a leading military power. December 7, 1941, has also become one of those days in history, when individuals remember where they were and what they were doing when they heard the news about the attack.

President Franklin Roosevelt called it "a day that would live in infamy," when he summoned Congress to ask for a declaration of war against the Japanese. And a united Congress and the nation rallied behind the war. Dalgo Bregoli was on duty at Pearl Harbor when the surprise attack occurred, and the memory of what took place that Sunday morning will never leave him. Bregoli was twenty years old when he enlisted in the Navy in 1939, believing that eventually the United States would go to war with Europe. Assigned to the U.S.S. *Perry,* a destroyer minesweeper stationed in San Diego, his unit was transferred to Pearl Harbor a year later.

Entering the harbor in the evening, he will never forget the sight of over 100 ships with their searchlights on. There were forebodings of events to come reflected in the growing military uneasiness. "In May of 1940 the Pacific fleet received orders to remain at Pearl Harbor indefinitely, and in the six months before the attack, we were required to have ammunition ready beside all guns." Yet two days before the attack took place, the U.S.S. *Perry* received orders to return to the States on December 8. The surprise Japanese attack changed all that and Bregoli became an eyewitness to a shattering historical event.

"I was on watch at 7:50 A.M. for the eight to twelve shift, when I happened to hear some planes overhead. The first two I thought had practice bombs, but when the third plane hit the hangar, I knew something was wrong. Then I saw the orange ball, the Japanese symbol of the Rising

Sun on the plane. After that all hell broke loose. A total of 353 Japanese planes, consisting of fighters, torpedoes, and high bombers attacked in two waves. The first wave of 180 planes came from 7:55 to 8:40 A.M. We thought it was all over, but five minutes later a second wave of 173 more planes came in. In addition to their planes, the Japanese also had five subs which carried midget subs.

"Since it was a Sunday, many men were off on liberty and none of the ships had a full complement. Also the ships were lined up, which was ineffective for firing, but who would think the Japanese would come 6,000 miles to hit us? Two ships away from us was the U.S.S. *Medusa,* which to me was the first ship to fire at the Japanese. We fought back with what we had available, our pistols and guns. My job was to be a first loader on the four-inch mounted guns that really could not be used for aircraft. We didn't have a carrier at Pearl Harbor when the attack occurred. And though our carriers were out at sea, they never chased the Japanese and I never understood why. The U.S.S. *Nevada,* a battleship, did start out after the Japanese, but fortunately the skipper beached her when she became damaged, and the channel remained open. If the Japanese had waited till the *Nevada* got into the channel before striking, she would have blocked the whole harbor.

"My ship was the first back into the harbor to sweep. And there was approximately four to five inches of oil on the water to clean. The final blow was all over

at 9:45 A.M. and anyone who says they weren't scared is lying. It was one hour and fifty minutes of hell." The staggering human loss and the extensive damage to the Pacific fleet was heartbreaking. There were 2,335 American servicemen killed that day and 1,143 wounded. In addition, 68 civilians were killed and 35 were wounded. The army and navy lost 188 aircraft and had 169 damaged. "The *Oklahoma* was overturned, the *California* sank straight down, and the *Utah,* a converted battleship, with 54 men aboard, was completely lost. The *Arizona* sunk when a bomb exploded and to this day entombs the bodies of 1,177 men."

Living through such an experience has become a shared bond that has united men long after the event. Pearl Harbor Survivors Units were formed with chapters throughout the nation, and Bregoli is active in the Massachusetts chapter, which meets monthly. Reunions have been held at Pearl Harbor every five years since 1966 and Bregoli attended in 1971 and 1976. "The saddest part is when you go over to the *Arizona* Memorial to pay respects to the men entombed there." Also tragic are the men who physically survive but were shell shocked during the attack. For them December 7, 1941, is forever.

And Then It Was D-Day

People of Western Europe: A landing was made this morning on the coast of France by troops of the Allied Expeditionary Force. This landing is part of the concerted

Peter Orlando, top row left, and shipmates at LeHavre, France, on V-E Day, 8 May 1945. (Courtesy of Peter Orlando)

United Nations plan for the liberation of Europe . . . I call upon all who love freedom to stand with us now. Together we shall achieve victory. (Broadcast by General Dwight Eisenhower, Supreme Commander of the Allied Expeditionary Forces, 6 June 1944.)

Of all the Allied offenses, the assault on Nazi Germany that began on the beaches of Normandy was the most stirring. "In war there is no second prize for the runner-up," said General Omar Bradley who commanded the American First Army. The impressive mobilization of 175,000 troops carried by 4,000 craft and supported by 600 warships and 11,000 planes was aimed at taking first place.

Peter Orlando was there in the channel waters, aboard a rescue tugboat, and the Bedford Street resident can remember well enough what it was like to be "five shades of white" on that day. "Nobody with me said anything about remembering this day for the rest of our lives. We were just plain scared and ill informed. All you heard were rumors and no one knew where we were going."

Orlando was twenty-two years old then, having joined the navy in October 1942 and was assigned as a radioman aboard the rescue tug U.S.S. *ATR2*. "We were part of the dungaree or working navy. There was no reluctance to enlist in those days. Instead the big fear was that you would be rejected. Everyone you knew seemed to be in the service." The ship was 168 feet long, 40 feet wide, and displaced 5,000 tons. Fifty men and six officers were aboard, that included divers, welders, shipfitters, riggers, radiomen, and firemen.

In the fifteen months preceding the invasion, Orlando and his crew were working in the English Channel ports, going from Folkstone to the channel ports as part of a convoy towing cement boxes called mulberries which were sunk to make two artificial harbors off the French coast. "It was like dragging an apartment house foundation behind you. Hitler was foiled by the beach invasions at Omaha and Utah, because he thought we would be landing at LeHavre and Cherbourg instead." Following the invasion when his ship did arrive at LeHavre and Cherbourg, the Germans had wrecked every facility. "It never seemed possible to the Germans that we could land on oceanfront property and they were never really committed there. Fortunately the German air force never materialized and we retained our air superiority throughout."

With the invasion originally set for June 5, the ships were sealed the night before but the seas became too rough because of a storm in the channel. "We only knew that we were part of an operation to get men on the continent. And after forty years what sticks in my mind is looking up at the mast and seeing the biggest American flag in my life. The morning of June 6, we sailed in a convoy between four and five in the morning. You could hear the sounds of the heavy guns from the cruisers and battleships trying to hit as many fortifications

as they could before the actual landings. By dawn the landings had started. The water was so rough that some landing crafts filled with water and with their heavy gear, many went down like rocks. We learned that we were at Omaha Beach and our job was to pull back into the sea any landing craft that were stranded. Landing ship tanks, called LSTs, that were found damaged and drifting off the beach, had to be blown up to stop them from blocking anything else trying to go by."

The fear of hitting a mine was an ever present danger that kept as many of his crew as possible staying topside. "When the U.S.S. *Mt. Vernon* transport hit a mine, we saw it go down like a rock. Some of the ships had barrage balloons shaped like sausages attached to them. If a German plane were to come too close, it risked getting a wing cut in the wire. Losses on the beaches were very heavy. The German artillery hidden in concrete pillboxes raked the beaches. We were giving as many landing craft as possible a chance to get off the beach and reload from the supply ships offshore. Otherwise, exposed on the beach, they were just sitting ducks. The only thing that made you feel good was that you had so much company. I never saw so many ships in my life."

A week after the invasion, he explains, the worst storm off the French coast in 100 years hit the beach, severely damaging the artificial harbors that were built. "We worked hard pulling off the ships that had lost their anchors or whose gear was broken. We worked off the beach for 100 days, getting our orders from a communication ship, the U.S.S. *Ancon*, anchored off Omaha Beach."

Thoughts of getting back home were always paramount. "The big thing on everyone's mind was making it back home." For Orlando that day came after Christmas in 1945. But there were shipmates not to be forgotten. One friend was Ivan "Curly" McGray. "He was an usher at my wedding and we have stayed in touch through the years. Every June 6 he calls me up to say, 'Hey, Pete, you know what today is?' "

The Homefront

During World War II, there were a series of towers in the area from which to spot enemy planes and Nashawtuc Hill was one of these, recalls Helen Shaw. "At the time you could see for miles around the hill and it was exactly four miles due west of Hanscom Field, which was a military airfield at the time, having been established in 1941.

"The towers were manned twenty-four hours a day on three hour shifts. There was a direct line to headquarters in Boston and every plane that the spotter saw was reported to the headquarters with its compass direction from the tower and which direction it was flying. These towers were placed on hills all around the coastline, and the ones in Massachusetts went as far

west as Peterborough, New Hampshire. We took a course in learning about the different types of planes, our own and that of the enemy. There was no such thing as radar in those days and we were a substitute.

"In winter it was very welcome to gather around the potbellied stove in the tower. The night shift must have been a lonely one. I had a morning shift and fortunately had a nurse to care for my five children. Our group of workers became great friends, and socially it was a very levelling experience. I can remember people who had been used to calling me, very politely, Mrs. Shaw, came to be on a first name basis with me. I think war does that sort of thing."

Eleanor Fenn remembers the efforts at recycling scrap metal and paper locally, collecting clothes for refugees, "bundles for Britain, we called them," and making bandages and other items for the Red Cross. "A canteen committee would be at the train station at seven in the morning to give the draftees going off to Fort Devens coffee and hot doughnuts often made by Mrs. Julian Ballou."

Frances Walker still has her Red Cross uniform, "my badge that tells I did a little bit during World War II." Walker was chairman of volunteer services and locally supervised all the committees that worked for the Red Cross during the war. "From 1942 through 1945 it seems that I lived on the phone. Those were very busy days for us organizing the Grey Ladies who served as volunteer hospital nurses, worked with the soldiers at the veterans hospitals, and started the blood bank at the First Parish Church. There was the motor corps who gave rides and the canteen to run. I went to countless meetings with service chairmen around the state and we were constantly soliciting people for all the jobs that were needed. And when the war ended, you don't just throw away your Red Cross uniform. It stays with you, like the American flag."

During the war, municipal operations were kept to a minimum, explains Bert Newbury, who was elected selectman in 1945. At the time Concord had three selectmen and being a candidate was "a very simple operation. There were no ads, maybe a letter or two in the local papers. The town report indicates that along with a population of 7,500, Concord had 21,000 chickens. And town reports were carefully read and referred to at town meeting. Town Meeting that year began at seven thirty and adjourned at ten minutes to nine, after voting on a total of eighteen articles. There was no bonded indebtedness and Schedule A, the appropriations schedule, was a total of $533,000. Government was a whole lot simpler then."

One of the articles approved divided the two voting precincts of Concord and West Concord into three, but the purchase of voting machines was defeated because of the expense. In 1945 Concord was a Republican town, and Newbury observes that while a relatively few uncommitted voters existed then, their increased numbers is a development of recent times. "The biggest change is that not only do the number of registered Democrats exceed Republicans, but that the number of uncommitted voters outnumber either party."

With the smaller scope of town government, Newbury remembers selectmen's meetings frequently being finished by ten in the evening. "In those days the townspeople picked out someone they had confidence in and then didn't tell them how to vote on each issue as it came up. There was not the constant direction. And serving in the days before the open meeting law, there were seldom any observers at the selectmen's meetings. The newspapers on occasion sent someone around to record action taken, but usually that was when some spectacular issue was at stake and not week by week. We felt perfectly free to suggest to anyone present that we would like to work in executive session. There was nothing sinister about this at all; it was an opportunity to match ideas one way and the other and finally come to a consensus of the board how we would vote on that issue."

Homecoming Time

Memorial Day in Concord has stayed as a hometown occasion and David Little is glad that the day belongs to the men who

---

The Grand Old Army of the Republic marches along Bedford Street. Circa 1910. (Printed from the glass plate collection of Barbara Bedell)

have served. "When I was in the Naval Reserves following World War II and marched in the city of Lowell's parade, the reviewing stand was loaded with politicians who had a great deal to say and it was pretty dreadful."

Little has been devoted to Concord's Memorial Day tradition since childhood. "It reminds me of a long-running play, the story doesn't change, just the actors. When I was a very small boy, I remember the horse-drawn barges carrying our Civil War veterans. I wondered then how anyone could fight a war if they were that old. It never occurred to me that they had once been young. People paid attention to them on this day, lots of attention, and they loved it."

Adeline Cabot goes back further in memory to when the soldiers of the Grand Army of the Republic marched proudly in a large contingent through the town. Among the Spanish American War veterans that Little recalls were Harold Tompkins and Thomas Todd, "two big burly men who just kept on going for a long, long time." World War I veteran Laurence Eaton Richardson, a devoted participant in many annual celebrations, observes that while the Civil War veterans for the most part still lived in Concord, this was less true of those from the Spanish American War and the parade served as a reunion for these men.

"No veteran was ever denied a burial because he was too poor," says Charlie Dee. His father James and Harold Orendorff lo-

cated all the graves of veterans on a map, making it easier to find and decorate them on Memorial Day. Richardson recalls the day as "more reverent and reflective than now," with the parade a serious occasion and decorating the graves of deceased veterans an important ritual. "The Concord Independent Battery used the horses that drove the ice cart and for a time fired a volley at the conclusion of the playing of taps when each new grave was decorated. When I began to march, the parade formed at the old armory and was led by a band, followed by Company I of the 6th Regiment, commanded by Ralph Peterson. It was an active day and one in which most people in town participated."

"Men like Laurence Richardson and fellow veteran Ripley Gage continued to look like soldiers in their uniforms long after many of the rest of us had gone to waist," adds Little. And such World War I veterans were young men when he first watched them go by as a boy. "They were very glad to be home and there was lots of horseplay in their ranks. It was a cheerful occasion to see them go by. They set a mood which said that though we weren't boasting about anything, by gosh we had been through it, had come home, and were making our way. And this was the time to do something in the memory of the people who were gone."

After World War II, Little joined the ranks of the marchers and watched these once jaunty veterans of the previous war "getting a little older and having a little more trouble climbing the hills to the cemeteries. It was a long haul for them. We started from the state armory and walked to Bedford Street, where the hill going up to St. Bernard's cemetery can be quite steep if you are marching." One such regular marcher among the World War I veterans was Bebe Hosmer, who throughout his life displayed his own irrepressible brand of individualism. "Bebe marched long after the doctors had warned him not to and had given up on him," recalls Little. "Towards the end of his life, we would get on either side of him and carry him up the hill. All the while he would be swearing something awful and we would be threatening to throw him in the swamp if he didn't keep quiet. During the last year of his life, he agreed to ride in the parade and hated every minute of it, and the next year he was gone."

For veterans who have moved away, Concord's Memorial Day celebration remains a time to keep in touch. General Otis Whitney was one such veteran who came up from Florida every year to march here. "There is a great feeling of comradeship to see these fellows who have moved away and whom you haven't seen since the previous year get together and hear them complaining how the street department has graded the hill on Bedford Street a little higher than last time. I don't know of any place else that does it quite like Concord." But Little cautions that Concord's special tradition will be lost if veterans don't turn out. "A lot of us are now beginning to worry about this."

21

A Time to Beat the Drums Slowly

Even death has its lore and its past within a town. It is a time to beat the drums slowly and reach out to tradition even as tradition itself changes. Visitors who come to see Concord often stop to wander among the old gravestones as if to feel the history that has come to rest here.

To Charlie Dee and the three generations of Dees who preceded him in Concord, these cemeteries have offered a continuity in the ever developing story of community life. His Bedford Street home and the funeral business there are the same as they were for his father and grandfather. Concord was a new start and a new life for Dee's great-grandfather Joseph, who arrived in 1860 from County Waterford, Ireland. Setting out by foot in Charlestown, he arrived in Lincoln to work at the Brooks farm. Eight years later, married with five children, he set out in a wagon with his family and possessions to farm Concord's land.

So much of Bedford Street was bog that the family had to cut through Bronson Alcott's backyard to reach the Fay farm that they had purchased. "I read in Thoreau's journals that he mentioned an Irish family had bought the Fay farm on Bedford Street. My great-grandfather combined being a gravedigger at Sleepy Hollow cemetery with farming." His son Joseph also dug graves for Willard T. Farrar, the town's first burial agent, who was appointed in 1868. Dee accepted Farrar's offer to join him in the funeral business and the Dee tradition of conducting funerals began following Farrar's death in 1910. For a time the death records of the town were those of the undertaker. In 1936, explains Dee, the WPA program under the New Deal financed the copying of card files from the Dee funeral home for the town.

Coffins were custom-made when Dee's grandfather worked for Farrar, and Farrar was also a cabinetmaker, which was common then. The funeral business grew, Dee explains, because the undertaker was asked to expand the care of the deceased. "People began to ask that he transport the coffin to the church and the cemetery as well as dig the grave and furnish the coffin." The hearse in each community was owned by the town, as the firetruck is today, says Dee. There were two wagon hearses within Concord. One was plain while the other was ornate with six big plumes on top with heavy black drapes. At the rear of the First Parish Church stood a row of horse sheds and the one with doors was the hearse house. Dee explains that this was later moved to the first gate of Sleepy Hollow. School House District #2, where Dee's grandfather went to school,

Charlie Dee's father, Joseph, drives the old
town hearse in the 1935 parade. (Collection of
the Concord Historical Commission)

became the cemetery's tool house. "My grandfather used it as a chapel with an organ inside. We still have the beaver hats, the coffin-making bench, and some of his brass-edged tools."

"When someone died," says Jim Powers, "it was of great concern to everybody in the neighborhood. At the Irish wakes we had, people made it a point that the body was never left unattended. The body would be in the living room, most of the women would be there and in the dining room, and the men would be out in the kitchen. Quite often there would be a bottle of whiskey in the pantry and people would help themselves to a little shot of it. Stories would be told out in the kitchen and there would be laughter, with no disrespect intended. It was a real family affair and death was accepted as something that had to be, but the deceased and the family were never left alone for a minute until the funeral was over. All the nationalities were in it together and had great concern for each other."

At a time when the town was small and people knew one another better, a death would be announced by tolling the bell at the First Parish Church. The bell tolled once for a man, twice for a woman, and three times for a child, and then tolled the age of the person. Dee remembers well the funeral of Gladys Hosmer in March 1970, because it was the last time that the town hearse was used. "She was an archivist and a local historian and it was her wish to be taken to her grave in the same hearse that took Thoreau, Emerson, Alcott, and Hawthorne. The driver and footman wore the old time funeral attire as the hearse drove from the Trinity Episcopal Church to Sleepy Hollow Cemetery through the streets lined with people. All you could hear was the clippety clop of the horse's hoofs while the bell tolled Mrs. Hosmer's eighty-three years."

22

The North Bridge and the 1956 Election Campaign

The rebuilding of the North Bridge and a presidential election campaign came together when Hurricane Diane struck on 18 August 1955, bringing record flood waters. The North Bridge suffered significant damage and was declared unsafe by state authorities.

"In the flood the pilings were damaged and swinging free so we immediately closed the bridge, which had been built of cement in 1909," explains Archie Ferran, who was then Chairman of the Board of Selectmen. "This gave us an opportunity to think of something that really looked like the wooden bridge that was there in 1775." Congress had declared this area of New England a disaster area and had appropriated the money to replace damaged property. But the North Bridge couldn't qualify in the category of a regular bridge since it led only to the Minuteman Statue with no road beyond. "So legally the North Bridge did not qualify for the use of the funds and also the communities west of

Concord had suffered tremendous damage so they were not too anxious about the North Bridge and figured the town of Concord could do a very good job on its own to replace it."

An official of the Commonwealth and the federal administrator of the disaster relief funds, however, seemed very eager for such monies to be allowed to rebuild the bridge, says Ferran. "I couldn't understand why they were in such a great hurry, especially as winter came on. John Volpe, who was then Commissioner of Public Works, came out here on a real cold blustery day and he wanted to have pictures taken at the North Bridge showing what we were going to do and Elmer Joslin and I met with him." But Ferran was not anxious to see another cement bridge. He and other Concord residents who favored the return to a replica 1775 wooden bridge promoted this through area newspapers and the story began to be picked up across the country. "Ralph McGill, who was then the editor of the *Atlanta Constitution,* wrote a magnificent editorial and other papers including the *San Francisco Chronicle* and the *New York Times* had articles on it, so we seemed to be winning."

A local Concord delegation met with then Governor of the Commonwealth, Christian Herter, and more publicity pictures were taken with him and Volpe. "Eventually through the Director of Public Relations for John Volpe, I was able to understand what lay behind the publicity. President Dwight Eisenhower had had a

September 1956, Governor Christian Herter
dedicates a newly rebuilt North Bridge. John
Volpe, then Commissioner of Public Works and
later governor, is seated; and Chairman of the
Board of Selectmen, Archie Ferran, stands besides the podium to the right of Herter. (Collection of the Concord Historical Commission)

heart attack and it was not known if he could run for a second term. John Volpe wanted to be governor and Christian Herter was willing to run for president in case Eisenhower was not able to continue. Herter's nomination for the presidential campaign would be touched off by the dedication of the North Bridge, rebuilt with federal funds. But Eisenhower recovered and was able to continue the campaign; Herter's chances of nomination were lost and the construction of the bridge slowed down. The dedication did finally take place in September 1956, and that's one very

few people knew about because to protect my friend, the Director of Public Relations, I kept it quiet.

"The wood used for the bridge was specially treated and supplied free of charge by a firm in Nashua, New Hampshire, called Koppers Coke. I was more or less laughed at and criticized when I said a wooden bridge, properly constructed, would last longer than one of cement. But I've held to the opinion that it will be there long after anything else that might have been built."

23

The Music School of Thomas Whitney Surette

For twenty-three years, students from across the nation came to Concord in the summer, as if in pilgrimage, to study music with Thomas Whitney Surette and his faculty. The Summer School of Music began in 1915 with 13 students and grew to its capacity of 180 students.

In the early years, the growing enrollment soon strained the capacity of Thomas and Ada Surette's double brick-ended home at 21 Lexington Road, and classes were moved to the First Parish Church and then to Concord Academy. Surette was born in 1862 into a large family, where each member played an instrument and music was regularly performed at the family home that is now the west end of the Colonial Inn. Among those who came to listen was Ralph Waldo Emerson, whom Surette viewed as "unresponsive, puzzled by the music, but like a true philosopher willing to learn." Surette would later serve as the organist at the First Parish Church, where he played at Emerson's funeral service.

One of his students from Concord, Katherine Davis, never believed Surette achieved the recognition due him in his hometown. Concord, Davis maintained, seemed preoccupied in recognizing its literary talents and failed to fully realize that Surette was also involved in the distribution of ideas. While by the mid-1920s Surette was a nationally respected musical scholar and educator, Davis sensed a certain skepticism from many of his townspeople who would muse: "Not Tom Surette? Louis Surette's boy? Why, he was just a boy who did odd jobs. We never thought he'd amount to much." Jackson Garrett, a friend of Surette's and a writer, concurred with Davis's opinion when he wrote that some of the townspeople sighed over Surette's "impractical pursuit of music," and thought he should go into some "gainful occupation." Yet Concordians did enjoy the performances of the light operas that he composed, such as *Priscilla* and the *Pilgrims's Proxy,* and when his students put on a concert, the church was filled.

Surette's ideas on the teaching of music became known through his writings for the *Atlantic Monthly,* his lectures at the Harvard Graduate School of Education, and his book, *Music and Life,* first copyrighted in 1916 and now published in paperback. Through his summer school he offered students "the daily experience of the best music, the union of substance with method, essential to all teaching. For method by itself is sterile." The tuition averaged fifty dollars and students could stay in rooms in private homes in Concord for as little as four to eight dollars a week.

Thomas Whitney Surette. Circa 1925. (Collection of the Concord Historical Commission, courtesy of Katherine Davis)

Katherine Davis, who later wrote and arranged music for Surette, recalls first coming to meet him in 1919. "I went to his house, trembling with respect. I found him taciturn and skeptical, letting Mrs. Surette keep the conversation going. Though at one point, I timidly said something about Keats and he perked up a bit. I began studying at his school in 1921. The

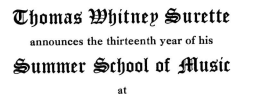

𝕿𝖍𝖔𝖒𝖆𝖘 𝖂𝖍𝖎𝖙𝖓𝖊𝖞 𝕾𝖚𝖗𝖊𝖙𝖙𝖊

announces the thirteenth year of his

𝕾𝖚𝖒𝖒𝖊𝖗 𝕾𝖈𝖍𝖔𝖔𝖑 𝖔𝖋 𝕸𝖚𝖘𝖎𝖈

at

Concord, Massachusetts

June 27 to July 22, inclusive, 1927

This School is for Teachers, for Students and for others who wish to increase their understanding of Music. It is not a Normal School. Its chief purpose is to develop the individuality of its students by bringing them in contact with great music, by dealing as clearly as possible with the principles underlying all art, and particularly the art of music, and to stimulate and help the teacher to work out, within those principles, his or her own way of teaching. Teaching is an art, not a science. To impose a rigid system on the teaching of any art is to destroy the art and the teacher.

The *Methods of Teaching used here are, therefore, much more free than are those used in most schools. And they have as a basis actual daily experience of the best music. This union of substance with method is essential to all teaching. Method by itself is sterile.

For those who are not professionally engaged in music the School offers a vivid contact with great music and a series of lectures and discussions on music and the other arts.

Mr. Surette lectures also on Literature (with special emphasis on Poetry) as well as on Education.

Three Chamber Music Concerts are given for the School.

---

*See "Music and Life" by Surette, chapters "Music for Children" and "Public School Music." (Houghton, Mifflin Co., Boston.)

Program of Surette Music School. 1927. (Collection of the Concord Historical Commission, courtesy of Katherine Davis)

Parish Hall accommodated over 150 students and it was comfortably filled. There stood two grand pianos and an orchestra of strings, made up of teachers and amateurs of unusual ability. Each session began with singing, and these people could sing! They were not here to train their voices, but to get a better understanding of their profession, the teaching of music. There is a slight pause, the baton comes down, and the room floods with the tide from that mysterious ocean of which music is the most perfect expression.

"Whether TW read a poem or talked about a book or a painting, he always sought to make us more conscious of beauty, wherever it might be, to change our awareness and thus our taste. Many students who had not before encountered such music or ideas felt criticized. There was for some of them a stage of resistance and even anger, which TW regarded as a healthy sign. To him the vaccination was taking." His publication of the *Concord Series* eventually included sixteen school books for students from kindergarten through high school, a set of piano books, a theory book, a hymnal, a book for home singing, known as the *Home and Community Song Book,* and the Harvard University Glee Club collection.

Ada Surette, who played the viola in the orchestra, was considered by the students to be an invaluable asset in the running of the summer school. She is remembered as a warm, energetic, and outgoing person. She took charge of arranging accommodations for the large numbers of students by calling on people in town to persuade them to rent a room. She is also remembered by Davis as being more tactful in handling any complaints that arose from a student or landlady. Davis recalls TW's "tart" reply when a student complained to him that there were flies in his room: "Take their names and addresses!" When Ada died in 1937, Surette tried to continue the school one more year without her. "It was a bad year and he did not try it again."

By the 1930s Surette's work was widely known and his students were placed in secondary schools and colleges from coast to coast. The Guggenheim Foundation asked that he judge the work of composers applying for fellowships, such as the young Aaron Copeland. But while he consented to do this, he generally discouraged composing among his own students. He was singularly devoted to the training of teachers who would serve to acquaint others with great music.

Indeed, Davis never showed him "a small piece" that she had written, the "Carol of the Drum," better known as the "Little Drummer Boy." The year the song was published, 1941, Surette lay paralyzed in a nursing home, where Davis visited him and where he died on May 19. He is buried at Concord's Sleepy Hollow. The following year his students filled the gallery of the First Parish Church and Davis remembers how "they sang with full hearts. Never had TW and Ada seemed nearer."

24
Concord's Little Drummer Boy

The carol "Little Drummer Boy" has become a classic, so synonymous with Christmas, many are surprised when they learn it was written as recently as 1941. Its composer Katherine Davis was living on Lexington Road at the time and had made a living for years writing music and verse.

"A new tune kept running through my head that seemed worth working on. I knew there ought to be a drum. I had known several French carols with a drum and was influenced by Ravel's composition 'Bolero' where the drumming begins softly and gradually gets louder and louder to its conclusion," says Davis. She decided to arrange the composition for a mixed chorus of voices where the basses and tenors would do the drumming. "I decided that I would build very slowly, and though the tune would go the same speed, the drumming would seem to get faster and faster." The words came easily to Davis and when she was finished, she "rather liked it. It sounded like a folk song. Well, where from? Why not from Czechoslovakia?"

Davis explains that it was an accepted practice for supposedly ancient folk tunes and long-time spirituals to be written by modern composers. " 'The Shepherd's Farewell' has been passed off as a very ancient tune but has such difficult modulations for the chorus to sing that it gives its age away. Elizabeth Barrett Browning's sonnets translated from the Portuguese weren't translations, but out of her own heart. I let mine be Czech and I called it the 'Carol of the Drum.' I put my name down as composer of the music for copyright purposes and then I realized I needed a translator for this 'old Czech carol' and so I made up the name C.R.W. Robertson." Davis adds that not only is the use of other names commonly accepted, it is sometimes urged by a publisher. "I had worked on verse for a school book series and I was encouraged to get some pseudonyms, otherwise it would look like I had written the whole book. All of my pseudonyms, be they made up or of deceased relatives, were duly registered." The procedure is described with the ease and acceptance of an actor's using a name other than his own for stage purposes.

The completed composition of the "Carol of the Drum" was first published by the B.F. Wood Music Company in Boston in 1941 and recorded by the von Trapp family of *Sound of Music* fame, "noted for their beautiful acapella singing." Wood, Inc., subsequently sold the business to a large publishing company in New York, Belwin Mills, Inc. "I was glad that eighteen years later Mills had a lot of lawyers to fall back on."

In December of 1959, a friend telephoned Davis to tell her that her carol was

Carol Of The Drum
(For Treble Voices S.S.A.A.)
a cappella

CZECH CAROL
*Freely transcribed
by C. R. W. Robertson*

KATHERINE K. DAVIS

"Come," they told me, Pa-

"Come," they told me, Pa-

Prum* prum, prum, prum, prum, prum, prum, prum,

Prum* prum, prum, prum, prum, prum, prum, prum,

rum-pa-pum pum, _____ "Our new born King to see, Pa-

rum-pa-pum pum, _____ "Our new born King to see, Pa-

prum, prum, prum, prum, prum, prum, prum, prum,

prum, prum, prum, prum, prum, prum, prum, prum,

SOPRANO I

SOPRANO II

ALTO I

ALTO II

PIANO
(for rehearsal only)

Moderato

Moderato

* Roll the R

"Carol of the Drum" sheet music. (Collection of the Concord Historical Commission, courtesy of Katherine Davis)

on the air all the time but was called the "Little Drummer Boy." When Davis heard the recording on the radio she found it to be "the most beautiful recording I could have possibly imagined, with only about two words different. You could hear it somewhere almost every five minutes. I must admit, it was very exciting and sort of disturbing to me." When she telephoned the radio station, she was informed that it was an old carol that had just been discovered. There were the names of four men on the composition and a different publisher as well.

Claim to this beautiful Christmas carol became a legal matter. Since there was no way for her to prove that she had actually written the carol and since the other men had spent enormous sums on promotion, it was decided to settle out of court. The song goes on in both versions, owned by Mills, and has been translated into other languages throughout the world.

Davis found that a sense of humor helped her accept her unasked for coauthors. "When one of these men held a lengthy interview with a Florida newspaper and referred to me as an old friend, the article was picked up and carried in a number of newspapers, including those in Boston. I called up Mills to ask if I could sass him a bit and was told it was good for publicity."

Katherine Davis spent a lifetime writing music and verse, but when the Christmas season comes each year, it is this carol that so many are indebted to her for writing.

25

The Joy of Christmas Past

The expectation of Christmas is a time for renewing traditions which are themselves altered by time. To many long-time residents, the beloved ritual of going out to the woods to cut your own tree and trimming it with stringed popcorn, cranberries, and other homemade decorations represented the special spark and warmth of the yuletide. An orange or tangerine placed in a child's stocking was considered a special treat.

The family of Gladys Clark celebrated Christmas in a simple manner, "for we were just farm folk. My two brothers would cut a cedar tree with berries, producing a lovely fragrance. We experienced great joy in decorating the tree with our popcorn and paper chains. On Christmas morning we awakened to a breakfast of oyster stew; and our big Christmas dinner would not be a turkey, but our own farm chickens with plum pudding. We did not give one another a lot of presents, but just received one good gift. It was a happy time together."

Elsie Loring Kennedy and Joseph Hay remember real candles on their trees,

while Peanut Macone describes the need for transformers to adapt the house current to a lower voltage for those using electric lights. Christmas was a special time at the Concord Reformatory, where Elsie's father worked. A movie would be shown and each man employed there was given tickets to attend. This was our opportunity to see a movie and we considered this to be "a big event, a real treat for us." The Loring family traditionally had goose for Christmas dinner, and an unwelcome byproduct for Elsie was the goose grease that her mother saved for medicinal purposes. "It was supposed to soothe your throat and was carefully given on a spoon or smeared on your chest." For dessert there always was a white fruitcake baked by Grandma Emery, who considering the equipment she had to use seemed to evolve the best way of doing things."

Joseph Hay's family generally cut their tree, a princess pine, from Annursnac Hill. "Scandinavians were big for Christmas. Back in the old country, the bleakness and darkness of the winter encouraged big Christmas preparations and celebrations. That was carried over here during the first generation. In our home, we had an extensive smorgasbord including pickled herring, lutefiske, which was a dried fish chopped up and soaked in water for one to two weeks and which I never liked, hogshead cheese, and other cold meats. I can still see the glow of the heated coals through the isinglass stove door in the parlor. There was a lot of singing in my family and my mother played the guitar

216   The Joy of Christmas Past

and my father, the ukulele. We all attended the Methodist church, which was then located at the corner of Thoreau and Hubbard streets, and later the West Concord Union Church."

Edith Bailey remembers Christmas in West Concord as a real community affair with sleigh rides, caroling from the West Concord Union Church, and Christmas mass at Our Lady's. Charlie Manion, who lived just over the Concord line in Acton and was a parishioner at Our Lady's, would walk the two miles to midnight mass there. Charlie Comeau recalls that in West Concord a tree, usually cut from Nashawtuc Hill, would be put at Dunn Square, at the corner of Commonwealth Avenue and Lawsbrook Road. "The tree would be decorated by a local organization, and the Christian Endeavor Society would often lead the caroling." As a teenager, Comeau earned money for college by working during the Christmas season in the West Concord Post Office. During the 1920s, the roads were still broken with horses rather than plowed. "I delivered the mail in the snow on foot and parcel post in a Model T touring car with running boards on the side. I frequently worked up to nine and ten o'clock at night, and people would sometimes invite me in for a cup of hot chocolate, which was greatly welcomed."

The stillness of a Concord Christmas. Circa 1900. (Courtesy of the Concord Free Public Library)

Gifts were fewer in number then, and for the most part were kept simple. "We didn't exchange presents outside the family," says Anna Manion. "There was no fancy wrapping paper, and our family used red or white tissue paper. Many of our presents were light enough to be placed on the branches of the tree while any big packages were placed underneath the tree and very few cards were sent out, compared to today." Her family attended St. Bernard's Church, which was smaller then, and the crèche was placed in front of the church. "A big part of Christmas for our family was going to church on Christmas Day, and after the mass, we children were given little boxes of hard candy."

Schools were alive with Christmas plays and pageants. Adeline Cabot captures the feeling of preparing to go on stage when she was one of the angels at Miss White's Home School for Girls on Belknap Street. "Draped in sheets, hands crossed on our breasts, our gilded cardboard halos hopefully in place, we recited one by one the 'Joys of Mary.' For days we transformed the room. There was the smell of pine as we arranged pine boughs and a wonderful feeling of expectancy. We all knew every line in the play and finding an understudy was no problem. I don't think I have ever had such a feeling of the spirit of Christmas as that pageant gave me from year to year."

The community sing around the tree in Monument Square has been a beloved tradition since the days when it was started by Thomas Whitney Surette, generally believed to be at the time of World War I. Harold Cabot remembers him "standing on the horse trough organizing the assembled people. One year he even tried to divide them up into tenor, alto, and bass sections, but this was not very successful." Eleanor Short, who studied with Surette, describes the Christmas sing as "awfully special. How particular he was in the way we pronounced the words. We would have a rehearsal two or three times down at the Town Hall so we would sing well by the tree on Christmas Eve." While the village people walked to the community sing, farm families like those of Gladys Clark rode to town on the horse and sleigh covered with buffalo robes to keep warm. "What a sight it was to see all those sleighs formed in a circle."

Arthur Motter Lamb, a master at Middlesex School, a choir director and organist, succeeded Surette as conductor of the sing. David Little remembers Lamb vigorously conducting and wearing a huge raccoon coat. "The children hoped he would fall off the horse trough because he really did leap around, but he never did." Donald Frothingham, a master at the Fenn School, who has continued the Christmas Eve tradition for the past quarter of a century, did fall off the horse trough one year into the snow. He delights in "the good feeling that just boils up out of the crowd and makes it such a beautiful occasion."

In the stillness of Christmas Eve, there is a special beauty to the town that Gladys Clark expresses: "Christmas Eve, a soft mantle of snow deepens the sanctity of the old burying ground on the hillside, enhances the classic beauty of the First Parish, magnifies the simplicity of the deserted Milldam, revives the quaintness of the Inn, and warms the hearts of carolers gathered about the yule tree on the village green who, within the hour, will go afield in Concord to sing of 'Peace on Earth, goodwill among men.'"

Index